GW00600742

THE LAND *of* LIGHT *and* PROMISE

50 Years Painting Jerusalem and Beyond
Ludwig Blum 1891-1974

THE LAND *of* LIGHT *and* PROMISE

50 Years Painting Jerusalem and Beyond

Ludwig Blum 1891-1974

BEN URI GALLERY
THE LONDON JEWISH MUSEUM OF ART
12 JANUARY – 24 APRIL 2011

The Art Museum for Everyone
The London Jewish Museum of Art, Bridging Communities since 1915

This catalogue is published on the occasion of the exhibition
The Land of Light and Promise: 50 Years Painting Jerusalem and Beyond
Ludwig Blum (1891 – 1974)
At Ben Uri Gallery, The London Jewish Museum of Art
12 January – 24 April 2011

Cover: *Jerusalem, View from Mount Scopus,* 1949
p. 2: *Jerusalem, inside the Walls, Looking East,* 1926
p. 11: Ludwig Blum, painting on a rooftop in Jerusalem

ISBN 978-0-900157-37-0

Catalogue
Edited by Anna Canby Monk assisted by Linda Gordon and Monica Kirk
Designed by Bheemla Harree
Produced by Tony Jackson
Printed by Abstract Group

Illustrations: Reproductions courtesy of the museums and private owners of
the works illustrated. The photographs were taken by or on behalf of Bonhams
London, Mira Chen, Ran Erde, Roy Fox, Avraham Hay, Elisha Katan, Lucien
Krief Gallery, Shlomo Seri, Tate 2010, Todd White.

The publisher thanks the copyright holders for permission to reproduce each
work illustrated. The publisher apologises for any omissions.

Acknowledgements

Dr. Dalia Manor, Curator of the Exhibition

Mira Chen, Michael Dak, Essayists

Diana Rubanenko, Translator from Hebrew to English

Logistics
Israel: Natalie Nesher Aman and Nathanael Breton of N&N Aman Gallery,
         Tel Aviv
UK: Suzanne Lewis and Anna Canby Monk of Ben Uri

Transport
Israel: Tapuz
UK: Momart

Thanks to Nelly and Natalie Aman from N & N Aman Gallery, who proposed
the idea of the exhibition and wholeheartedly supported with their knowledge
and expertise.

The exhibition would not have happened without the deep involvement and
generous support of Olesia and Leonid Nevzlin. We are grateful to them and
appreciate their awareness of the significance and historic value of Ludwig
Blum's artistic heritage.

Dr. Dalia Manor, Curator of the Exhibition would like to thank the lenders to
the exhibition and expresses her sincere gratitude.

Special thanks to Geula Goldberg and Gila Cohen of Beit Hatfusot, The
Museum of the Jewish People, Tel Aviv for their important advice and
assistance; to graphic designer Nomi Morag for her kind collaboration; to Ira
Dolgina for her support behind the scenes; to Nathanael Breton of N & N
Aman Gallery for the logistical help in transportation.

The curator in her research for this exhibition benefited from the knowledge
and expertise of Ram Ahronov and Gideon Hermel, and is grateful to all other
individuals and institutions that helped during the initial research towards the
Ludwig Blum exhibition held at Beit Hatfutsot Museum in 2009. As always,
Mira Chen, the artist's granddaughter supported the project with enthusiasm
and helped all along.

CONTENTS

SHORT HISTORY AND

Founded 1st July 1915 by the Russian émigré artist Lazar Berson at Gradel's Restaurant, Whitechapel in the East End of London as 'The Jewish National Decorative Art Association (London), "Ben Ouri"'. The name echoed that of legendary biblical craftsman Bezalel Ben Uri, the creator of the tabernacle in the Temple of Jerusalem. It also reflects a kinship with the ideals of the famous Bezalel School of Arts and Crafts founded in Jerusalem ten years earlier in 1905.

Ben Uri Gallery is Europe's only dedicated Jewish Museum of Art working in partnership with secular and Jewish museums in the UK and internationally.

The gallery and museum is an educational institution dedicated to enhancing the quality of life of all whom it impacts. It embraces a new broad and fully inclusive role for museums in today's society and addresses contemporary issues through art and its social history.

By fostering easy access, greater appreciation and both social and academic enjoyment of the visual arts, there is an ongoing opportunity to demonstrate its value as a robust and unique bridge between the cultural, religious, political differences and beliefs of our fellow citizens.

Its purpose is to enable the largest possible audience, drawn from the widest possible communities from both home and abroad, to explore for inspiration, learning and enjoyment, the work, lives and contribution of British and European artists of Jewish descent, placed where relevant alongside their non-Jewish contemporaries, within the artistic and social context of the national cultural heritage.

Children's visits to and activities at the museum are free of charge.

Its principal route to achieving this is by enabling broad and straightforward physical and virtual access through location, publication, Internet and outreach to the following:

- THE PERMANENT COLLECTION: Consisting over 1000 works the collection is dominated by the work of first and second generation émigré artists. The largest of its kind in the world, it can be accessed physically or virtually via continued exhibition, research, conservation and acquisition.

- TEMPORARY EXHIBITIONS: Curating, touring and hosting important internationally-focused exhibitions of the widest artistic appeal

MISSION STATEMENT

which, without the museum's focus, would not be seen in the UK.

- PUBLICATIONS: Commissioning new academic research on the artists and their historical context to accompany the museum's exhibitions.

- LIBRARY AND ARCHIVE: A resource dating from the turn of the 20th century, documenting and tracing in parallel the artistic and social development of the Ben Uri and Jewish artists working or exhibiting in Britain as part of the evolving British historical landscape.

- EDUCATION & COMMUNITY LEARNING: For adults and students through symposia, lectures, curatorial tours, publications, library research; for children through focus related lessons, visits, after school art club, family art days and competitions. Children always free at Ben Uri!

- SCHOOLS: For local, national and special needs schools through artists' visits and the museum's path-finding 'Art in the Open' programme, which designs teaching modules using the museum's collection as part of the national curriculum.

- ARTISTS: Monthly artists peer group programmes, Ben Uri International Jewish Artists of the Year Awards competition, Guidance and affiliation benefits.

- CARE IN THE COMMUNITY: A pioneering project, 'Art as Therapy' addresses the needs of the elderly by practising artists.

- WEBSITE: Providing an online educational and access tool, to function as a virtual gallery and artists' reference resource for students, collectors and scholars.

The strength of the museum's growing collection and the active engagement with our public – nationally and internationally – reinforces the need for Ben Uri to have a permanent museum and gallery in the heart of Central London alongside this country's great national institutions.

Only then will the museum fulfil its potential and impact the largest audiences from the widest communities from home and abroad.

FOREWORD

For the first time since being exhibited in London at the Royal Academy, the Fine Art Society and Ben Uri in 1938, we are proud to bring the art of Ludwig Blum back to the United Kingdom for his first European Museum survey.

The exhibition traces the career of the Czech born Israeli topographical artist Ludwig Blum, who immigrated to Palestine in 1923 and settled in Jerusalem at the age of 32. He was classically trained; first as a young talent under David Khon in Vienna and then, after serving in the First World War, from 1919 at the Academy of Fine Art in Prague.

This exhibition of some 35 works traces Blum's consistent representation of 'the real' over half a century of painting the Holy Land and beyond. Jerusalem was Blum's city and he never ceased to find inspiration in its architecture, holy places, markets, peoples and the extraordinary changes of light and shadow, which bathes its buildings each day of each season.

Blum's European persona and academic practice never changed in the heat and heart of this very different continent. He is recognised not only as a distinguished artist of the classic mould but also as the finest topographical artist of his time working in the Levant. His was a unique period in history being the 25 years before and after the founding of the State of Israel in 1948. He travelled extensively and across borders to Iran and Iraq, and his work chronicles in realistic and archival fashion the characteristics of different societies during those times.

The exhibition brings together a remarkable body of Blum's work not seen in London since he exhibited in London in 1933 and 1938. Included are a set of remarkable views of Jerusalem, its landscape and peoples, providing a unique historical glimpse of this majestic and holy city over half a century. Alongside are rare views of building sites during the early construction of the city of Tel Aviv as well as scenes in Iran and Iraq from 1930, Kibbutz Kiryat Anavim west of Jerusalem from 1932 and Kibbutz Degania on the Sea of Galilee from 1934, farming and new industrial developments highlighting the diversity and contrast with city life in the '50s and beyond.

When viewing Blum's style and palette, his concerns with space and colour, his swift brushwork and sophisticated conveying of the effects of light you will notice a synergy with the landscapes of Palestine by London based American painter John Singer Sargent. The same can be said when comparing Blum's 1920s panoramas of Jerusalem with those of British artist David Bomberg, who similarly arrived in Jerusalem in May 1923 and painted his now celebrated series between 1923 and 1927. Given that Blum was in London in the early twenties before immigrating to Palestine, they were both Europeans living and painting in a new city and climate, and they painted from similar viewpoints and in similar styles, it is perfectly likely they knew each other.

There are many that deserve public recognition for their part in the very complicated mosaic required to present such an exhibition particularly when it is an international collaboration.

Our first tribute must go to Nelly Aman who has dedicated her life to promoting the visual arts in Israel and has long championed the art of Ludwig Blum. The combination of an artist we knew and admired and Nelly Aman's vision and advocacy proved irresistible and Ben Uri and you, our visitors, are in her debt.

Transforming vision into reality requires a fully committed and positive thinking team working together as one combining organisation, passion and good humour to best present the art and scholarship on Ludwig Blum to new audiences in the West. In London the team was led by Suzanne Lewis and Anna Canby Monk and in Israel by Natalie Nesher Aman and Nathanael Breton and their individual and joint expertise and dedication overcame every obstacle.

There are few words that could accurately reflect the contribution to this exhibition by our Curator, the distinguished art historian Dr. Dalia Manor. Her scholarship on Blum is renowned and her most recent book 'Art in Zion, The Genesis of Modern National Art in Jewish Palestine' is essential reading for students of this period. We thank her.

I equally thank our catalogue team led by Editor Anna Canby Monk, Designer Bheemla Harree, Proof readers Ingrid Posen, Marion Cohen and Sue Glasser and Producer Tony Jackson who translates their vision into this reality. I thank the family of Ludwig Blum for their unreserved support and granddaughter Mira Chen for her reminisces in the catalogue. Our thanks to the distinguished journalist and author Michael Dak for his insights and contribution to our understanding of Blum's Jerusalem. We thank Marie Magdalena and Jan Bureš and all at Ceskà Televize for their spirit of partnership in granting permission to show their documentary on the artist.

Without the understanding and support of our lenders, being prepared to be without their prized paintings for close to six months and most at a distance of 3,500 km, there would be no exhibition and we pay great tribute to them.

Finally we pay a special tribute to the passion and vision of collectors Olesia and Leonid Nevzlin. Both demonstrate their commitment to the visual arts out of a realisation of the social, learning and historical values that art generates in today's fast changing celebrity focussed society. Their commitment is to creativity being oblivious to race, religion or privilege. They encourage learning and creativity at every level. They believe in the art of Ludwig Blum and recognise the place of Israeli artists within the broader Western artistic context. We share their beliefs.

Ben Uri is proud to provide the opportunity to Western audiences to discover the majesty of Blum's practice and travel with him on an extraordinary topographical journey some 73 years after his last exhibit in London.

David J Glasser

Co-Chair (Executive)

Ludwig Blum
1891–1974

1891	Born 24th July in Líšeň, near Brno, Moravia
1910–12	Vienna: Private art lessons with David Kohn. Gymnastics training
1913	Recruited to the Austrian Army
1914–18	Serves in the Austrian Army during WWI
1919–20	Prague: studies at the Academy of Fine Art. Active member of the Maccabi sports club
1921–23	Visits Amsterdam, London, Paris, Spain and Italy
1923	Immigrates to Palestine, settles in Jerusalem
1924	Marries Dina (Clementine) Mayer, birth of their daughter, Dvora
1925	During a first visit to Brno, exhibits his works. In the following years continues to visit and exhibit in Czechoslovakia and Europe
1926	Birth of his son, Eliyahu (Elie)
1930	Travels to Iraq with Wolfgang von Weisel
1936–37	Spends some months in Brno, Czechoslovakia
1937	Commissioned by Museum of Biblical Antiquities in Brno to paint a panorama, *Jerusalem, a view from the Mount of Olives*. The painting is exhibited in Blum's studio and the Tel Aviv Museum prior to its delivery
1938–39	Lives in London for 18 months, paints portraits and participates in exhibitions
1946	Son, Elie Blum, is killed in action during the Night of the Bridges, a Palmach operation
1948-49	Volunteers for the Civil Guard in Jerusalem, guards roadblocks, draws and paints figures and sites of Israel's War of Independence
1951–52	During a ten-month visit to the USA, exhibits and forms professional contacts
1955	Publishes the album, *10 Historical Sites of the Holy Land*
1964	Death of wife Dina
1967	Awarded the title of honorary citizen of Jerusalem
1974	Dies in Jerusalem, 28th July

Portrait of a Country: Ludwig Blum Paints the Land of Light and Promise

Dr. Dalia Manor

Portrait of a Country:
Ludwig Blum Paints the Land of Light and Promise

Painter of Jerusalem

'Painter of Jerusalem' is the title inscribed under the name of Ludwig Blum on a commemorative plaque on his native house in Pohankova Street, Brno-Líšeň, in the Czech Republic. It is probably not unusual for a Painter of Jerusalem to have been born in Central Europe. In modern history and in Jewish history in particular, it is not unusual for people to have gained fame and success far away from their country of origin. It is also not unusual nowadays for countries, especially in Central and Eastern Europe, to reclaim their Jewish heritage and to honour the achievements of Jewish artists who were born there as part of their own cultural legacy. The plaque on the house where Blum was born was unveiled in 2000. Five years earlier, the museum in Brno, the Moravská Galerie, displayed an exhibition of his work followed by an exhibition at the Franz Kafka Centre in Prague from the collection of the Jewish Museum in Prague. In 1998, Czech television produced a film on the life and art of Ludwig Blum, and today Blum is listed among Brno's famous people on the city's official website.

Ludwig Blum's relationship with his native country however is by no means the familiar story of posthumous honour. Many Jewish artists who emigrated from Eastern Europe in the late 19th century and early 20th century to Paris, New York or England severed their ties with their birth place and established themselves as artists in their new countries. This is also the case for most Jewish artists who emigrated to Palestine. Yet, Ludwig Blum always kept his old and new homelands close to his heart. A self nominated ambassador for Jerusalem, he was at the same time a citizen of Czechoslovakia until the demise of the republic with the invasion of Nazi Germany in 1939. Long before travel abroad became easy and convenient, long before artists would run a career in more than one country, Ludwig Blum travelled back and forth between his two homelands, painting in one, exhibiting in the other and feeling at home in both. 'Between two homelands' is a term often used in relation to German Jews who came to Palestine in the 1930s, forever longing for the life and culture of the Fatherland, which had expelled them. The pain of the two homelands – as the poet Leah Goldberg phrases it, a sense of a torn identity – is perhaps a feeling shared by immigrants all over the world. But it became more acute because of Zionist expectations that immigrants would develop a sense of belonging to their new home and leave behind their previous lives in the Diaspora.

As far as we can tell, Ludwig Blum was not concerned with such identity issues; first and foremost because he came to Palestine in 1923 out of a sincere commitment to the Zionist ideology and immediately fell in love with Jerusalem. Moreover, he was able to continue his ties with his family and with his native country where he found a supportive public for his art. His art was the motivation behind his frequent travels, and also a means by which he could identify himself as belonging both to the Land of Israel and to the rest of the world. In terms of the ongoing dispute in Israeli art between two desired orientations, the local and the universal, Ludwig Blum could define himself through his painting as being simultaneously local and universal. This multifaceted identity was possible perhaps because Blum ignored the

major ideologies that were competing with each other in the field of Israeli art. One required the adoption of the language of western modernism, chiefly the influence of Paris, which was conceived as the path to universalism. This had been manifest since the late 1940s in abstract art. The other was the strongly manifest drive in the 1920s to create a genuine Eretz Israeli art which would reflect the national will for cultural regeneration in the "old new" homeland.[1] The so called 'Eretz Israeli School' of the 1920s expressed these aspirations in the choice of subject matter and styles. Although at the time Blum was close to this trend in his selection of landscapes and local types, he was considered foreign to the major tendencies in Israeli art because of his non-modernist approach to art.

Ludwig Blum regarded himself as an academic painter and this was how he presented himself throughout his career. During the 20th century the term 'academic' was associated with traditionalism, even conservatism, which evidently positioned him outside the mainstream of modern Israeli art. Blum's classical technique and brilliant skill, his search for beauty in nature and his naturalistic treatment of it, along with his disregard for such modernist values as originality and self-expression, cast him in the role of outsider. Thus, he was equally admired and criticised.

"Since Blum knows how to easily paint what he sees, with relative freedom of execution," Mordechai Narkiss, the director of the Bezalel national museum wrote in 1935, "there is a danger in this ability for the common viewer –

who enjoys the look of things that are 'really like in life'". The critic praises Blum's technical skills in drawing, composition and colour, which other artists lack, "but somehow all that repels the onlooker. It seems that things are too polished; they want to be more real than real".[2] In 1951, the poet and critic Yeshurun Keshet remarked on the documentary quality of Blum's painting and the virtuosity of its execution. He commended Blum's artistic creative power, yet found in the sheer academicism the cause of imbalance and an occasional lack of emotion, even where the artist had absorbed Impressionist influences.[3] In the 1960s, when the perpetual demand for the "New" seemed to be ruling the art world, the stability and consistency of Blum's painting was appreciated: "when everything changes (and not always for the best)," wrote art historian and critic Avraham Ronen, "Blum's style is an exceptional phenomenon … almost a rare 'nature reserve' – the academic naturalistic style, a kind of last century version, par excellence".[4] Indeed, being so far removed from the art of the time, as Haaretz critic Michael Sgan-Cohen observed, the naturalistic depiction of landscapes and historical and national events was not only strange to, but entirely outside, modern art discourse, leaving the critic to admire Blum's mastery of academic painting technique and to trace his art back to19th century Orientalism.[5]

If his style seemed to belong to a different era, his subjects were often tuned to the 'here and now' of his place in Jerusalem and many other sights around the country. His sense of belonging to his beloved city, which in 1968 granted him the Honorary Citizen of Jerusalem title, was complemented by his confidence in his art and its long roots in the cultural tradition of Europe. Ludwig Blum's Jerusalem, the city that is dear to so many people in the world, Jews and non-Jews alike, is the key to his strong sense of identity as an artist who belonged to

Jerusalem as much as he belonged to the world that cared about Jerusalem.

From Moravia to Jerusalem

Ludwig Blum was born on 24 July 1891 in the Moravian village Líšeň (Lösch) in the vicinity of Brno (Brünn), the capital of Moravia, then part of the Austro-Hungarian Empire. Today, Líšeň is one of the districts of Brno in the Czech Republic. Blum's parents, Philipp Caleb Blum and Maria (Miriam) née Kohn both had long roots in Moravia. It was not uncommon at the time to see Jews living in tiny communities in villages and small towns throughout Moravia. Observing Jewish tradition and daily life within a Christian environment, however, was not a simple task for a single family like the Blum family, which at the same time tried to integrate into village culture as much as possible. Ludwig Blum's recollections of his youth, as reported in an autobiographical summary,[6] were of healthy and happy times. With his brothers and local village friends, he climbed trees, rode the farmers' horses to swim in the river, roamed the countryside and woods and collected flowers, butterflies and birds. Ludwig was especially talented in gymnastics and trained with his brothers in the backyard of their house. Later on he competed successfully in gymnastic competitions – his expertise was on the high horizontal bar. From a young age Blum demonstrated talent and interest in drawing and painting.

Around 1910, he went to Vienna to study art. The capital of the Empire was a hub of intellectual creativity in philosophy, psychology, art, architecture and design. Jews from the Czech lands and other regions achieved prominence there in the arts and science as well as in trade and industry. There he received private tuition from the Jewish Viennese academic painter David Kohn (1861–1922) for about three years. In 1913, he was

Fig. 2 Ludwig Blum in uniform of the Austro-Hungarian Army, c. 1918

drafted into the Austrian army for a year but with the outbreak of World War I in the summer of 1914 he was called up and served until 1918. As a staff-sergeant in the light infantry, Blum served on the Italian front for a year and was later transferred to headquarters where he served as a war artist. The war was a hard time for the Blums: all the sons and sons-in-law were conscripted. Blum's older brother, Isaac, was killed in 1915 on the Russian front. A few months later his brother-in-law was killed on the Italian front leaving his sister Regina widowed with three children. Another brother, Hans, was taken prisoner of war by the Russians, returning home only two years after the war ended in an appalling condition. The younger brother, Robert, was injured during the war.

After the war, as the Austro-Hungarian Empire broke up, the first Republic of Czechoslovakia was established. The Jews of Czechoslovakia, comprising less than 2.5 percent of the overall population, played a major role in the country's economy and culture – far beyond their numerical strength. The country not only recognised the Jewish community but also offered them political rights of representation in parliament in a Jewish Party.[7] Tomáš G. Masaryk, the founder and first President of Czechoslovakia, was unprecedentedly supportive of Jewish nationalism, including Zionist settlement in Palestine. In 1926, Czechoslovakia established diplomatic relations with Mandate Palestine, opening a consulate-general in Jerusalem and, in 1927, Masaryk himself came to visit.[8] The cultural, social and economic strength of Czechoslovak Jewry during the interwar years and the warm relationship between Czechoslovakia and Jewish Palestine were a significant context for Ludwig Blum's activity and success during those years in and between the two countries.

Fig. 3 Ludwig Blum (second from the right) with fellow gymnasts, 1920s

After the War, Blum resumed his studies in Prague at the Academy of Fine Arts under the guidance of the academic painter Franz Thiele (1868–1945), receiving his diploma in July 1920. Blum's ideas on art were deeply-rooted in the European classical tradition, which he set out to see after his studies at the Academy. From 1921 to 1923 he travelled back and forth between the great artistic centres of Western Europe, including Amsterdam, London and Paris, adding Spain in 1922 and Italy in 1923. Occasionally, he returned home, but spent most of that period in museums and historic monuments, observing, drawing and painting. In May 1923, Blum embarked on a ship from Sicily that took him to Palestine.

Blum's Zionist sentiments were forged during his years in Vienna and especially in Prague, where he became deeply absorbed in Jewish and Zionist writings. In both cities Blum engaged in his favourite sport of gymnastics and in Prague he was in charge of this sport in the district's Maccabi club. Blum's Zionist ideals and sporting interests often intersected, and in September 1921 he attended the Twelfth Zionist Congress held in Karlovy Vary (Karlsbad) in Czechoslovakia.[9] It was the first Congress held after the War and after the Balfour Declaration and one where the founding of the Maccabi World Union was proclaimed. Some years later, Blum designed the poster for the Maccabi games held in 1929 in Moravská Ostrava (Mährisch Ostrau) in Czechoslovakia. Blum himself, now 38, participated in the games as a gymnast, representing Maccabi Jerusalem.

When Ludwig Blum settled in Palestine, he was part of a wave of Jewish immigration known as the Third Aliyah. Some of the most illustrious individuals who would shape the cultural, social and political life of the future State of Israel immigrated during those years, among them poets and writers, theatre people, architects, scholars, political leaders and artists. The 1920s and 1930s were a highly significant period in the formation of the field of Israeli art. Ludwig Blum joined the local cultural milieu but for many years he aimed his art at audiences abroad, exhibiting in Berlin, Amsterdam and London and above all in his country of origin, Czechoslovakia.

Shortly after his arrival in Jerusalem, Blum met his future wife Dina (Clementine) Mayer (1882–1964), a highly educated and qualified nursery-school teacher who had emigrated from Germany in 1914. In March 1924 they married and in October of that year their daughter Dvora was born. In 1926 their son Elie was born.

Blum was enchanted by the country instantaneously, as he wrote in his memoirs. It was the landscape of Jerusalem, the endless space, the Judean desert and the mountains of Moab with their unique colours that put a spell on him. Blum joined the Hebrew Artists Association and took part in its Annual Exhibition held April–May 1924 at Migdal David (the Citadel). This exhibition gained a reputation as a significant moment in the local art field, marking the rise of a group of modernist artists. It became clear to Blum, who by then was already married and expecting a child, that the art market in Palestine would not meet his needs and it was time to turn to the overseas market. In the spring of 1925, together with his wife and baby daughter, Ludwig Blum travelled to Czechoslovakia and held a one-man show at the Artists' House in Brno. He wrote in his memoirs that the show was so successful that none of the seventy oil paintings displayed would be shipped home. Subsequently, Blum returned to Europe every couple of years, travelling and exhibiting in two or three venues each time. On his own terms, Ludwig Blum was making an international career for himself.

Exporting the Land of Promise

Views of the Holy Land, especially of Jerusalem, were the core of Blum's repertoire: panoramic views of Jerusalem seen from Mount Scopus or the Mount of Olives, the Wailing Wall, the Tower of David, the Valley of Kidron, and Rachel's Tomb in Bethlehem. Other images added an exotic flavour of alleys and gates of Old Jerusalem populated by colourfully clad figures. He also painted portraits of Oriental 'types', Arabs and Jews. Many of the landscapes of those years are executed in quick and long brush-strokes. The tones tend to be cool, creating the sense of early morning light. At the same time he also developed his topographical naturalism in depicting the city's architecture.

Blum also painted sites that are particularly significant for Christians: the Via Dolorosa, the Church of the Holy

Fig. 4 *Jerusalem, Damascus Gate*, 1928

Sepulchre, the Garden of Gethsemane, Bethlehem and Capernaum by the Sea of Galilee. Blum's audience was mostly Jewish, but Christian feelings about the Holy Land brought him important commissions. In 1926, he prepared a series of paintings of different sites in the Holy Land to be printed and distributed in the Netherlands accompanied by texts. Ten years later, a Catholic society in Czechoslovakia commissioned a monumental panorama of Jerusalem, which remained a source of great pride to him.

Beside his classical images of the Holy Land Blum also painted and exhibited abroad the 'new' Palestine and the Zionist enterprise; Degania – the first kibbutz, Migdal – the agricultural colony near Tiberias, the farm of Kinnereth, all three by the Sea of Galilee. He painted a pioneer woman (Chaluza) feeding chickens, an orange grove and Kyriat Anavim, the first kibbutz in the mountains of Jerusalem. In Jerusalem Blum also painted views of the newly established Hebrew University on Mount Scopus and in Tel Aviv the new neighbourhoods and construction sites of the rapidly growing city.

Palestine, in the painting of Ludwig Blum, is a mixture of Jewish, Christian and Muslim sites; a country loaded with history and ancient monuments, where new urban and rural life is emerging; a country rich in topographical features, from the desert and the Dead Sea, through mountains and valleys, to the Sea of Galilee and the Mediterranean.

Jerusalem, however, was Blum's major theme, and panoramic views his speciality. His most ambitious painting was the large-scale panorama commissioned for the Museum of Biblical Antiquities in Brno. Information about this commission was published in the press in December 1936:

> Ludwig Blum, the Jerusalem artist who recently returned from a successful trip abroad, has received a remarkable commission from the museum at Brno (Czechoslovakia). He is to paint a Jerusalem panorama, as seen from the 'Dominus Flevit' chapel on the Mount of Olives. The picture will be 8 metres in length and 2 metres in height. When completed it will be exhibited both in Jerusalem and Tel Aviv.[10]

Blum first painted a 'small' version (50 x 188 cm) in the open air and then enlarged it to scale in a large hall provided for him at the Jerusalem YMCA. Within less than four month, by late March 1937, Blum put the finished panorama on display in the yard of his studio. The Czechoslovakian consul was the guest of honour and many visitors flocked to see the wonder. The scale of the painting was an important factor in the publicity it received. After a tour to the Tel Aviv Museum the painting was sent to Brno. In February and March 1938, the Jewish press in Prague, London and Palestine reported that the panorama was ready at its destined location.[11]

Fig. 5 Ludwig Blum works on the Jerusalem Panorama, 1937

The small panorama was shown at the London Royal Academy in 1938, probably in the annual exhibition. It was selected by the artist and author Wyndham Lewis in a list of his personal choice, which he published on 30 April in *The Star*, by then a well established and popular London newspaper. Of all the reviews of his work, it was this recommendation of his showing at the Royal Academy that Blum mentioned in his memoirs and on many other occasions.

Fig. 6 *Jerusalem, View from the Mount of Olives,* 1936

A few weeks later, Blum opened a private exhibition at the home of Mrs. Benzion Halper in London's Maida Vale. The widow of the distinguished Hebraic scholar, Mrs. Halper used to host events in support of Zionism. The *Jewish Chronicle* reported that Blum's exhibition of 'Palestine Paintings & Portraits' was opened by Sir Ronald Storrs, the former Governor of Jerusalem, and by Mrs. I. M. Sieff with Lady Fitzgerald in the Chair. These

Fig. 7 *Portrait of Sir John Chancellor, The High Commissioner*, 1930

two aristocrat Jewish women were active in fundraising for Zionist projects and other Jewish causes. The portraits of the hostess Mrs. Halper and of Lady Fitzgerald were especially praised.[12]

Blum was quite effective in attracting the support not only of dignitaries in the Anglo-Jewish community but also some high-ranking officers in the British army who were linked to the Mandate in Palestine. Five years earlier, in 1933, Blum exhibited at the Wertheim Gallery in London. Among the notable guests who attended the opening were the Czechoslovakian ambassador to Britain, Jan Masaryk, the renowned diplomat and son of the first President of the Republic, Viscount and Viscountess Allenby – the famous General Allenby who conquered Palestine in the First World War – and Sir John and Lady Chancellor, the former High Commissioner of Palestine. Their portraits, painted during Chancellor's service in Palestine, were on display. In 1940 Blum painted the portrait of Sir Harold MacMichael, the High Commissioner from 1938 to 1944. Apparently Ludwig Blum remained on good terms with British Government officials until the end of the Mandate in 1948, regardless of the political situation.

In the summer of 1938, the family joined Blum in London and the children, now in their teens, went to a boarding school in Sussex. But they were unhappy there and were transferred to schools in Hampstead where the Blums were then living. By that time, in late September, the clouds of war were gathering over Europe. In London fear of the pending war was intensely felt and was reflected in Dina Blum's letters to her sister in Jerusalem.[13] Many of the Blum's acquaintances had already left town as she wrote. In January 1939, she and the children returned to Palestine.

Earlier in October, the threat of imminent war seemed to be over and it was replaced by some optimism. Ludwig received portrait commissions after a long period without work. In December, his small panorama of Jerusalem and a couple of other Jerusalem landscapes were exhibited alongside Abel Pann's biblical characters at The Fine Art Society in London. The verisimilitude that characterises Blum's painting provided a realistic context to Pann's romantic depictions of biblical figures, invoking typical responses like that expressed in *The Jewish Chronicle*: "It is one of the astonishing things about Palestine that life is lived there very much as it must have been lived four thousand years ago".[14] The prevalent Western belief that the Orient had never changed through the centuries was reinforced by the Orientalist painters of the nineteenth and twentieth centuries who visited the Holy Land and looked for images of people and places that verify the scriptures.

Blum and British painters of Palestine

One of Blum's popular subjects was a panoramic view of the desert of Judea and the Dead Sea with the mountains of Moab in the background. At times the scene includes a caravan of camels or figures of Bedouins in the foreground. In its purest form the image is a vast empty landscape, comprising four horizontal strips: in the foreground the desert is in light brown, or darker browns for shadows created by setting sun. The thin strip of the blue waters of the Dead Sea intersects the desert and the pink mountain ridge in the distance. The sky in the upper horizontal strip gradually changes from pink-orange to yellow and light blue.

Fig. 8 *View of the Dead Sea,* 1945

In its composition and colour scheme, Blum's desert panorama bears a surprising resemblance to a painting by the London based American painter John Singer Sargent (1856–1925). Sargent painted *The Mountains of Moab* in 1905 while on a visit to Palestine and Syria. Other paintings by Blum also bear a remarkable resemblance to some of Sargent's paintings of Palestine landscapes. It is hard to tell if Blum encountered *The Mountains of Moab* (which was in a private collection until 1957), but during his time in London in the 1930s it is likely that he had the opportunity to see other Sargent paintings. Sargent's works at the Tate Gallery were

Fig. 9 John Singer Sargent, *The Mountains of Moab,* 1905

displayed in the new Sargent Gallery, which opened in 1926. Over twenty paintings – mostly portraits and a few Italian landscapes – were on display.[15] Blum, who was rather sceptical about new trends in modern art, might have found in Sargent, the successful society portrait painter, a perfect model to follow. Whether or not Blum was knowingly influenced by Sargent, he was mentioned as a follower by a reviewer of his 1933 London exhibition. *The Scotsman* commented on Blum's "swagger brushwork and comparatively 'photographic' vision" and added:

> Blum is an accomplished painter with a sweeping Sargentesque style … His power of conveying the sense of glare and heat is astonishing. He creates the feeling that his sun-soaked canvases would be warm to the touch like a radiator.[16]

The similarity between Blum's and Sargent's desert paintings may be the work of nature: the pinkish purple colour of the mountains of Moab and the sky above them at sunset is a view seen and painted by various artists, notably William Holman Hunt in *The Scapegoat* (1854–5). Blum's style and palette, his concern with space and

Fig. 10 *Portrait of Dvora, the artist's daughter aged fifteen,* 1939

colour, his swift brushwork and sophisticated conveying of the effects of light bring him closer in many ways to Sargent's Impressionism and especially to his paintings of the Holy Land. Where Blum shows a fairly direct influence of Sargent was in portraiture. A portrait of his wife wearing a hat (1944) reflects the kind of elegant and theatrical portraits characteristic of Sargent. A portrait of Blum's teenage daughter Dvora with her pets (1939) and other portraits of children also disclose his debt to Sargent.

Blum's paintings of Jerusalem in the 1920s, especially his views inside the Old City are intriguingly close to another British artist, David Bomberg (1890–1957). It is hard to establish if there was any contact between the two artists and it may be a mere coincidence that both Bomberg and Blum arrived in Jerusalem in May 1923. Blum was still at the beginning of his career and he came to settle. Bomberg was a successful radical modernist who had experienced a crisis in his art after the War and travelled to Palestine as a way to help him find his artistic direction, and also to provide a livelihood. His Palestinian paintings, mostly landscapes based on observation painted between 1923 and 1927, are regarded by scholars as a transitional period.[17] Painting from nature in and around Jerusalem, Bomberg's style became gradually more topographical, and as Richard Cork put it, "he began to view Jerusalem as a strangely pristine city, free not only from people but from any sign of the dirt, decay and architectural impurity…".[18]

Fig. 11 David Bomberg, *Jerusalem, Looking to Mount Scopus*, 1925

Compared to many other artists who portrayed Jerusalem, Bomberg was unusual in the angles he chose for his views, among them the sections of the Old City from rooftops, which he painted in 1925. Were Blum's rooftop views of the Old City inspired by Bomberg? Blum's large *Jerusalem, inside the Walls, Looking East* of 1926 can be compared to Bomberg's 1925 *Jerusalem, Looking to Mount Scopus*.

Fig. 12 *Jerusalem, inside the Walls, Looking East*, 1926

The difference is as obvious as the similarity. Blum's view is panoramic, trying to cover as much width and depth as the eye can reach, conveying an accurate depiction of each and every building. His goals appeared to be fidelity to the visual experience and giving the viewer the sense of actually standing in the same place. Bomberg's roof vistas are often cut narrow and he used vertical compositions. His topographical rooftop views demonstrate a deliberate focus on geometrical form and structure resonating with his earlier more abstract works.[19] Blum painted Jerusalem many times but his rooftop view of 1926 is quite exceptional.

Fig. 13 *Tel Aviv, View towards Jaffa,* 1927

In the following years he painted a few panoramic rooftops views of Tel Aviv. Bomberg's contact with the local art community of Jerusalem was limited. They probably had little knowledge of Bomberg's previous achievements. According to artist Yossef Zaritsky, who knew Bomberg at the time, he had no influence on local art and never showed what he did to the other artists. He visited Zaritsky's home when other artists were present, but since he knew no Hebrew and hardly any Yiddish, communication was limited.[20] Bomberg was not supportive of Zionism, was primarily engaged with British government officials and had little in common with the Jewish community in Palestine. Whether Blum was able to see any of Bomberg's paintings or whether Bomberg saw any of Blum's is not known. They might have met while painting out of doors in Jerusalem. Blum might have seen Bomberg's works at some of the British officials' redidences, such as Norman Bentwich, the Jewish Attorney-General who acquired the work *Jerusalem, Looking to Mount Scopus.* In any event, several of Blum's paintings of 1926–27 share some of David Bomberg's artistic concerns.

Among the artists who created visual images of Palestine, the best known is undoubtedly the Scottish artist David Roberts (1796–1864). During his 11 months' long journey to the Near East in 1838–9, including the Holy Land, he made numerous sketches of biblical sites. Based on these he then produced books with lithographs that were published in the 1840s to much demand and acclaim. Roberts often exaggerated the landscape features and his inaccuracy was criticised by 19th century scholars. In spite of these faults his works were very popular and widely circulated.[21]

Fig. 15 *Fountain of Job,* 1925

Fig. 14 David Roberts, *Fountain of Job, Valley of Hinnom,* 1842

Blum clearly knew David Roberts' work. We know of at least one painting in which he copied one of Roberts' lithographs: a 1925 watercolour *Fountain of Job.* He titled it in English, very unusual for Blum who normally used German script when titling his painting. Apart from difference in colours and in the proportions between the building and the surroundings Blum's watercolour follows every detail of Roberts' composition, including the three figures in the foreground. Copying other artists' work had been a common practice especially in the academic tradition. Blum also used photographs as a source for his paintings. We do not know why he copied Roberts' lithograph, particularly as the site itself is of little significance. Bir

Ayub is traditionally identified with the biblical fountain of Ein Rogel, and today is located inside a mosque in the Silwan village, near Jerusalem. By the time Blum painted it the site must have changed over the century since Roberts painted it. This raises further questions about Blum's practice and intentions. Perhaps he regarded Roberts' images of the Holy Land as a guide in selecting the sites to be painted for Christian clients, such as the paintings he made for a Dutch publisher in 1926.

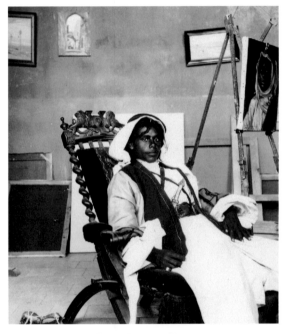

Fig.16 Model in the artist's studio, 1920s

Ludwig Blum's relation to these British artists demonstrates that his interest in views of the Holy Land was not merely that of a 19th century Orientalist. He hardly ever painted biblical scenes and concentrated instead on landscapes, topographical views and architectural features of holy places. His Orientalist scenes in his early years in Jerusalem were close in spirit to other Jewish artists in Palestine at the time, portraying exotic Arabs, Bedouins or Yemenite Jews, or incorporating them into street scenes in the Old City. For Blum these people were a natural part of the scene rather than a manifestation of life that had remained unchanged since antiquity.

Art at a time of war

Throughout the 1920s and 1930s Ludwig Blum retained his status as a Czechoslovak citizen.[22] In February 1921, his first passport was issued in Brno and in 1930 the Czechoslovak consulate in Jerusalem issued him a new passport registering his children as well. But in March 1939 Czechoslovakia ceased to exist and Blum – now in London – had to return to Jerusalem where he received a British Passport of Palestine. He immediately left for Britain to resume his work, but not for long. With the outbreak of the Second World War in September 1939, Blum returned to Palestine.

As Blum's professional ties with Europe were now severed he lost his major markets and source of livelihood. For over a decade he would have to sell his paintings locally. In his attempt to establish himself in Jerusalem, Blum turned to British Government officials. In October 1940, a small item in the social section of the *Palestine Post* announced that Blum's portrait of Sir Harold MacMichael was about to be finished and displayed. The copy was probably submitted by the artist with the hope of gaining new clients. Long before PR became part and parcel of the art world, Blum was regularly feeding the press – primarily the Jewish press – with information about his practice, social standing and professional achievements. Items in the press include a reported visit by the deputy High Commissioner to Blum's 1934 exhibition, information about his 1938

London exhibition and the dignitaries who had attended, and a mention of a painting by Blum given as a gift to King Gustav of Sweden in 1945.

In August 1944, ten years after his previous one-man show in Palestine (apart from the Panorama display in 1937) Ludwig Blum held a solo exhibition at the Menorah club in Jerusalem, a club for veteran soldiers where exhibitions were occasionally held. A review of the exhibition noted Blum's characteristic "amiable optimism" with an atmosphere of "a cheerful cool spring morning or equally enchanting rose-red dusk" that pervades his landscapes. "It is never hot in Blum's Palestine" he remarked on an exhibition held in the height of summer.

> Any foreigner seeing these views of splendid settlements amidst green pastures, these panoramas of romantic historical towns, would want to pack his trunk and set out on a pilgrimage.[23]

Blum's serene, idealised views appealed to foreigners seeking to take home a visual memento from the Holy Land. Among them were Australian soldiers who served in the British Army and British officers who attended the Menorah club. Postcards series that Blum printed in the 1930s and 1940s had a similar purpose.

By the end of World War II, with growing disappointment in British policies towards Jewish immigration, the active struggle against British rule in Palestine took the form of a series of underground operations coordinated by the Jewish Resistance Movement. The largest of these, conducted by Palmach units on the 16–17 June 1946 is known as the Night of the Bridges. It aimed to destroy eleven bridges around the country that linked Palestine with neighbouring countries and so damage both the reputation of the

Fig. 17 *Frank, Volunteer Soldier from Canada*, 1949

British army and the legitimacy of the British Mandate rule. Blum's son Elie was one of the fourteen fighters killed in the operation on the railway bridges over the Achziv (A-Ziv) in Western Galilee. Ludwig and Dina were devastated. The absence of a grave to weep over (the bodies' remains were buried in a mass grave in Haifa) made the tragedy even harder to bear, as Dina wrote. Only in the 1950s was a memorial erected on the site where the fighters fell. A remembrance ceremony takes place there annually.

As true believers in the Zionist cause and undeterred by their personal loss, Dina and Ludwig Blum became volunteers in the Jewish Civil Guard that was established in Jerusalem in 1947 to maintain public order during the long siege of the city. Blum also started to paint fighters and soldiers, battlefields and the destruction caused by war. In April 1948, he asked permission to visit and draw battle sites, citing his earlier experience as a war artist. To this he added a pledge to personally contribute to the national struggle for independence: "Present need requires me to lend my talent and my knowledge to the people in its great and holy war", he wrote.[24] Some months later, the operational officer of the Jerusalem Brigade granted him a permit "to visit our positions or their vicinity … for the purpose of executing his art works (war scenes, etc.). All required aid should be given to him."[25] In November, Blum visited the frontlines in the south of Israel, and painted in Kibbutz Negba and in

Fig. 18 The artist in his shell-damaged studio, 1948

Be'er Sheva. His main focus though was, as always, Jerusalem. After having painted the city's splendours so many times, he now depicted the impact of war: the Italian hospital and the church in the Notre Dame pilgrim centre in ruins, the explosion on Ben-Yehuda Street and rubble in Kibbutz Ramat Rachel. Even Blum's own studio was damaged by a shell.

Driven by his deep commitment to the national cause, Blum continued lending his paint and brushes to major historic events after war. He painted the first sitting of the first Knesset (Israeli parliament) in February 1949 and in August that year he attended and painted the ceremonial burial in Jerusalem of the remains of Theodor Herzl,

"the Visionary of the State". In 1951, he painted the gathering of the Twenty-Third Zionist Congress in Jerusalem, the first held in the State of Israel. Blum's version of history painting was remote from most mid 20th century art. This was especially the case in Israel, where pre-modern artistic genres were virtually absent.

Exploring new territories

The establishment of the State of Israel brought not only pride and joy but also serious social and economic difficulties. In 1949, an austerity policy was pronounced and in 1951 Israel suffered a severe economic crisis. For an artist like Ludwig Blum, who was entirely dependent on sales of his paintings, this meant that he had to travel abroad again. This time it was to America. In 1951, Ludwig and Dina Blum left for a long stay in the United States. Blum exhibited in New York and the east coast, mostly in venues related to Jewish or Zionist organisations and some Christian ones. In later years he continued his contacts with American collectors and dealers and occasionally also exhibited in Europe.

During the 1950s and 1960s Blum continued to visit and paint his favourite views around Israel: Tiberias and the Sea of Galilee, the Bay of Haifa, Acre and Achziv, Safed and Nazareth and views in Tel Aviv. In Jerusalem, however, many of his preferred views were now beyond reach, on the other side of the border. Blum continued to paint some of his successful themes – panoramic views, a street market or a dark alley in the Old City – using his previous paintings as models. This was not a new practice for him. Blum regularly repeated his motifs and images, revisiting and painting the same site time and again. But he also used to copy his own paintings, creating original replicas in different sizes and formats. This practice is not unusual among modern artists although rarely discussed in analyses and historical writing.[26]

Fig. 19 *Nazareth*, 1958

Fig. 20 *Haifa Bay*, 1951

Blum also looked for new sights in Jerusalem to replace his images inside the Old City. He found them in the alleys of the Jewish Orthodox neighbourhood of Mea

She'arim, and in Nahalat Shiv'a, two of the oldest of Jerusalem's neighbourhoods built in the 19th century outside the ancient walls which still preserved the flavour of the city of old. Colourful fruit and vegetable markets were also among his themes in the 1960s. For views of Jerusalem's Old City Blum had to choose new viewpoints from the border zone on the western part of the city looking towards the city walls. In his last years Blum also painted views from the rooftop of his house in the centre of Jerusalem.

Fig. 21 Ludwig Blum paints Mount Zion and the walls of the Old City of Jerusalem, 1930

Travelling throughout the country, he added the southern desert areas that became part of the new State and depicted sites and projects showing economic and industrial development. Much like his early days when he painted agricultural settlements, in the 1950s Blum painted the developing resort town of Eilat by the Red Sea, the magnesium plants at Sedom, near the Dead Sea and not far from Eilat the ancient site of Timna. There he was equally attracted by the majestic natural stones known as 'Solomon's Pillars' and the newly built copper mining facility, a project that gained much publicity and was a source of national pride. Blum must have been spellbound by the wilderness of southern Israel. Yet, he did not hesitate to incorporate into these primordial landscapes facets of modern life and industrial progress. In his representational painting of both landscape and human intervention in it, Ludwig Blum was poles apart from his Israeli artistic contemporaries. Their landscapes were frequently a point of departure towards abstraction.

A Romantic Classicist

Blum was often regarded as a Master, a term signifying respect for his technique and skill. But it located him in an unspecified past, in the realm of the classics and the 'old' masters – far-off from contemporary Israeli art that aspired to become part of twentieth century international art. In his style and themes Blum operated outside modern art movements, a choice that gained him the admiration of the general public more than that of the art establishment and the critics.

More than any other artist of his generation Ludwig Blum depicted, in a vibrant naturalistic manner, Israel's ideals and achievements in 'real-time': from the pre-state agricultural settlements, to the War of Independence, state symbols and industrial development, all carefully chosen to enhance historical significance. Nonetheless, it was his pictures of the Holy Land that made his name and linked him to the tradition of Orientalist painting. No doubt he was enchanted by the country and some of his images follow the Holy Land views as formulated by

visiting European artists. But Blum was no visitor. He returned to paint the same sites time and again throughout his life, and not only the famous places but also less familiar scenes. Blum's painting offers a variety of Jewish, Christian and Muslim holy places but his focus was not religious sentiment. He was interested in space, light and colour. If the viewer was to be enchanted, it was not necessarily due to the biblical context, but thanks to his virtuosity in creating the illusion. The landscape in Ludwig Blum's painting is not a stage for an ancient narrative in the footsteps of the patriarchs and saints; it is the place itself, as seen by a twentieth-century viewer. Unlike the 'authentic' biblical landscape sought out by many nineteenth-century Orientalist painters, Blum's topographic naturalism allows changes and contemporary buildings to enter the frame and become part of the landscape. Ludwig Blum was not seeking an imaginary past but observed the present and the future of the country where he lived and which he so loved. His idealism and optimism is reflected in many of his works, in the folkloric street scenes, the brightness of the colours in his landscapes, and in the bravura of handling the paint. Positioned outside the trends of the 'Now' and the 'New' Ludwig Blum can nowadays be rediscovered: a painter of outstanding qualities, who created unique landscapes of diverse and original views, and whose works still look fresh and captivating to the contemporary viewer.

Dr. Dalia Manor, Curator of the Exhibition

Notes

1   For a full discussion of the formation of Israeli art in view of the Zionist ideology see: Dalia Manor, *Art in Zion: The Genesis of Modern National Art in Jewish Palestine,* London and New York: Routledge, 2005.

2   Mordechai Narkiss, 'Blum's exhibition', *Davar,* 11 January 1935. [Hebrew] Translation from the Hebrew texts and hereafter are the author's own.

3   Yeshurun Keshet, 'Exhibitions in Jerusalem,' *Haaretz,* 2 March 1951. [Hebrew]

4   Avraham Ronen, 'Exhibitions in Jerusalem,' *Haaretz,* 7 June 1963. [Hebrew]

5   Michael Sgan-Cohen, 'Ludwig Blum,' *Haaretz,* 28 April 1967. [Hebrew]

6   Ludwig Blum, 'Statt einer Autobiographie,' *Zeitschrift für die Geschichte der Juden,* Tel Aviv, no. 2/3, 1966, pp. 103–110. For a fully detailed biographical description see Dalia Manor, *The Real and the Ideal: The Painting of Ludwig Blum,* Tel Aviv: Beit Hatfutsot, Museum of the Jewish People, 2009.

7   Livia Rothkirchen, 'Czechoslovak Jewry: Growth and Decline (1918–1939)' in Natalia Berger (ed.), *Where Cultures Meet: The Story of the Jews of Czechoslovakia,* Tel Aviv: Beit Hatfutsot and Ministry of Defence Publishing House, 1990, p. 107.

8   Ibid., pp. 110–111.

9   A return travel permit issued by the Zionist Congress office is kept among Blum's papers together with many letters and documents at the Central Zionist Archive (CZA) in Jerusalem, A423/2.

10   *Palestine Post,* 14 December 1936, p. 2. Similar information was published in Davar, 17 December 1936, p. 8. Blum informed his wife of the commission in a letter dated 14 October 1936, CZA A423/6. The actual dimensions of the painting are a little smaller than publicised: 196 x 746 cm, as documented in the Biblical Museum inventory. I am grateful to Magda Veselská of the Jewish Museum in Prague for providing me with this information. Blum's panorama is still at the Augustinian Monastery in Brno where today is the Gregor Mendel Museum of Genetics.

11   *Die Welt, Jüdische Illustrierte Zeitung,* 15 February 1938, p. 1; *Palestine Illustrated News,* February 1938, p. 1; *The Jewish Chronicle,* 18 March 1938, p. 26.

12   'Ludwig Blum's New Paintings', The Jewish Chronicle, 3 June 1938, p. 44.

13   Noga Stoler-Galun (ed), *The Road Taken: Dina Mayer-Blum,* 1882–1964, Jerusalem, private publishing, 2007, pp. 81-85. [Hebrew]

14   'Abel Pann and Ludwik [sic] Blum', The *Jewish Chronicle,* 2 December 1938, p. 55.

15   The Sargent Gallery was open until 1939. I am indebted to Christopher Bastock of Gallery Records at the Tate for the detailed information about the Sargent Gallery, provided via email, July 2009.

16   'London Art Shows: Eurich and Blum', *The Scotsman,* 13 April 1933, p. 11.

17   Richard Cork, 'Bomberg in Palestine: The Years of Transition', in *David Bomberg in Palestine 1923–1927,* curator: Stephanie Rachum, The Israel Museum, Jerusalem, 1983, pp. 5–19.

18   Ibid., pp. 14–15.

19   Ibid., p. 15.

20   Quoted in Stephanie Rachum, 'David Bomberg: Views from the Jewish-Zionist Side', in *David Bomberg in Palestine 1923–1927,* p. 24.

21   Yehoshua Ben Arieh, *Painting the Holy Land in the Nineteenth Century,* Jerusalem: Yad Izhak Ben-Zvi, 1997, pp. 99–102, 105.

22   Blum's birth and residency certificates were issued and re-issued several times during the 1920s and 1930s, probably for purpose of citizenship rights: CZA 423/2

23   Theodor Friedrich Meysels, '*Paintings and Woodcuts*', Palestine Post, 22 August 1944, p. 4.

24   Letter from L. Blum to Headquarters, Jerusalem, 26 April 1948, *tzayar milhama* (war artist). IDF Archive 582/4944/1949. I am indebted to Shai Hazkany who brought the existence of this letter to my attention. Blum made several drawings of the Castel hill on the road to Jerusalem shortly after its conquest in a hard and bloody battle in April 1948. This experience may have led him to make an official request.

25   The permission is dated 6 August 1948, CZA A423/36.

26   The case of Giorgio de Chirico, who painted numerous replicas of his own famous paintings, was put to the test in an exhibition held at the Estorick Collection in London in 2003. It raised controversial responses in the art press.

Jerusalem

Jerusalem, View from Mount Scopus towards the Valley of Jehoshaphat, 1924, oil on canvas, 49 x 59 cm

Jerusalem, inside the Walls, Looking East, 1926, oil on canvas, 81 x 140 cm

Walls of Jerusalem, 1926, oil on canvas, 40 x 50 cm

Jerusalem in Snow, 1927, oil on canvas, 41 x 61 cm

Church of the Holy Sepulchre, 1928, oil on canvas, 38 x 46 cm

Jerusalem, Temple Mount, 1928, oil on canvas, 33 x 45 cm

Grove of Olives, Gethsemane, 1928-30, oil on canvas, 31.5 x 46 cm

Mural Sketch for the Artists' Ball, c.1934, watercolour and pencil on paper, 27 x 47 cm

Temple Mount and the Western Wall, 1943, oil on canvas, 32 x 46 cm

Jerusalem, View from Mount Scopus, 1944, oil on canvas, 33.5 x 60 cm

Jerusalem, View from British Government Palace (Armon Hanatsiv), 1948, oil on canvas, 59 x 72 cm

Jerusalem, Notre Dame in Ruins, 1948
Oil on canvas
60.5 x 50 cm

Jerusalem, View from Mount Scopus, 1949, oil on canvas, 73 x 116 cm

Jerusalem, View of Sultan's Pool and the Citadel, 1960, oil on canvas, 50 x 73 cm

Mea She'arim neighbourhood, Jerusalem;
View of Ein Ya'akov Street, 1960
Oil on canvas
61 x 46 cm

The European Jerusalem of Ludwig Blum

Michael Dak

The European Jerusalem of Ludwig Blum

Ludwig Blum was a committed Zionist and in 1923 he left Europe for his new spiritual home in Jerusalem. Blum was – and remained – a European but Jerusalem was his city and he painted it continuously for 50 years.

The Zionist dream was in part to transform the vision of the Jewish prayer "L'Shanah Habah B'Yerushalayim" – "Next year in Jerusalem" – into the reality of a Jewish state in the biblical lands of their forefathers. Many reflected this was a four and a half thousand year old dream but the Zionist movement, led by Theodor Herzl, captured the imagination of Jewish peoples across Europe and enthusiasm grew increasingly in the last decade of the nineteenth and early decades of the twentieth century.

Everyone's individual dreams were different. Herzl's was of the big picture and saw Viennese-style café life as a part of this new diverse society with European culture – consisting of opera, white gloves, evening dress, bow tie, top hats – being just as natural in the heart of the Middle East as in Vienna or Berlin.

Fig. 1 Viennese café scene

Fig. 2 Theodor Herzl

Fig. 3 Franz Kafka

Fig. 4 Gustav Mahler

Herzl, the visionary who called the first international Zionist conference in 1897, wrote about his dream of the Altneuland – the Old New Land. Published in 1902, the book saw the return of the Jewish people to their biblical homeland as an independent state flavoured with the best of European society as he saw it.

Kafka, the writer, dreamt of settling down with his 'last love' Dora Diamant. He dreamt not of Opera or top hats but of opening a European café restaurant in Haifa with Dora as chef and himself as the waiter.

Composer Gustav Mahler, although baptized and no Zionist, wrote "in the Austro-Hungarian Empire I am a Moravian, in the German sphere I am an Austrian, and I am a Jew in both."

The stimuli for those who engaged with Zionism were many and rooted in history, but the contemporary was as much about identity and belonging as it was about anti-Semitism or religious freedom. Individuals like Herzl from Budapest, Kafka from Prague, Mahler from Jihlava and Blum from Líšeň, (today is part of Brno in the Czech Republic) all belonged to the German speaking cultural milieu (Deutscher Kulturkreis) and found comradeship in this vision.

By 1923, when Blum arrived in Jerusalem, the British Mandate had already taken over the administration of Palestine from the collapsing Ottoman Empire. European émigrés were encouraged that a British colony would make the cultural landing somewhat easier and so it seemed at least in these early years.

Palestine under the British began to emerge after centuries of Ottoman rule. Jerusalem, however, was the exception in the area and had started its awakening and emancipation some sixty years earlier with the arrival of hospitals, missionaries, pilgrims, convents, authors, photographers and artists.

These were formative years for the population of Jerusalem. Architectural by-laws (such as mandatory use of local stone for building in Jerusalem) set a different tone than the previous Ottoman "bakshish" system.

The thirties saw an ever-growing need for asylum for Jews fleeing persecution in Europe but Palestine did not open its doors wide; refugees were met with obstacles and quotas by the British authorities. For many of those who did make it through, Jerusalem was not the classic pioneering vision embodied in their Zionist ideal. The city already had a growing and established infrastructure and central government, with hospitals, tourism, academies, the Bezalel School of arts and crafts contrasting sharply with the barren lands and villages to the north or desert to the south.

Alongside the British government agencies were those 'in waiting' centred on the headquarters of the Jewish agency, which led the aspirations for the "Old New" homeland.

Herzl's foresight proved completely accurate in the respect of culture as European Jews brought their engagement with all brands of the arts with them to Palestine. This was the platform for Europeanism in this small enclave of the Middle East that sustained itself throughout the twentieth century before and after the founding of the State of Israel in 1948.

Whilst lifestyles varied, language was universal. Hebrew as a living language started blooming towards the end of the nineteenth century. It was slowly evolving from a language confined to prayer and religious learning in the Diaspora into a contemporary language and a modern alternative to the dominant central and eastern European language of Yiddish. In the 1920s and 30s a hectic debate took place in Jewish Palestine about language. Even the choice of language in academic teaching was under scrutiny.

Hebrew became the language of modern Jewish Palestine but it was neither universally embraced nor guaranteed. Herzl was far from convinced that the Hebrew revival would prevail. He thought that German rather than Hebrew or Yiddish would be the language of the Promised Land, "It is impossible for us to converse with one another in Hebrew. None of us would have sufficient command of Hebrew to buy a railway ticket. Each one of us will speak in his own language."

Reading Hebrew was no easy task. Hebrew is written from right to left, which exacerbates the difficulty of acquiring fluency. Many immigrants found it very hard to acquire a decent knowledge or even conversational fluency. Their German accent gave their origins away to their last day as a foreigner.

Like so many other émigrés language proved a serious challenge for Blum and his family. In an article written for a Jewish German magazine in 1929, Blum's wife, Dina Mayer, wrote about cultural assimilation in Palestine:

Well. The first problem is language. Woe if you don't speak Hebrew. You will not starve, of course, because every hotel and every hostel know the strangest languages on earth. And there are cobblers, and there are workers using all languages of the world, Germans, French, English, Armenians, Italians and others. But you are far from intellectual life, all lectures are held in Hebrew, theatres appear only in Hebrew, newspapers are written in Hebrew [...] and of course there are the children, all of them without exception, speak Hebrew and they demand it from their environment.

Herzl was right with regards to European culture but mistaken on European language.

Blum's Jerusalem was European and he never gave up his European persona in dress or artistic style.

Some argue Jerusalem post 1920 itself was as much European as Oriental as the British followed by the European Jewish immigrants created a seamless mix of cultures. They say even the acquired Orientalism was European. It was so European that it was hard to peel off the cultural layers and listen to, let alone blend into, the local sounds and colours.

A revealing example is many years later, when Israel's broadcasting service inaugurated its Arabic broadcasts; the identification tune was the Bacchanale from Camille Saint Saëns' opera "Samson and Delilah".

This epitomised the European concept of oriental music, perhaps reminiscent of the depiction of the Orient in the paintings of the European masters.

Language and cultural issues aside the darkening clouds over Europe in the 1930s brought more and more Jews of German origin to Palestine. Many of them settled in Nahariya, Haifa and Jerusalem and some in Tel Aviv and Ramat Gan. They were labelled "Yekkes".

There is some debate as to the etymological origin of the term: one version has it that their inflexibility caused the "locals" to call them Y.K.H ("Yehudi Kshe Havana") meaning "a Jew hard of understanding". A more lenient version claims that they were labelled "Yekkes" because of their habit of wearing a jacket ("Jacke") even on the hottest summer days.

Although originally the term was reserved for Jews from Germany, it came to embrace the cultural presence of Central Europe. Ludwig Blum's jacket, eternal bow tie and brimmed felt hat, were a clearly identifiable part of "Yekke" Jerusalem.

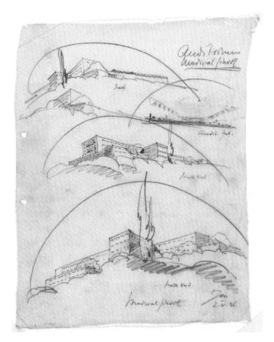

Fig. 5 Erich Mendelssohn, Hebrew University, Hadassah Medical Center, Mt. Scopus, Jerusalem

The true Yekke neighbourhood was Rehavia, just a short stroll away from the centre of Jerusalem. Many buildings were commissioned from the famous Yekke architect Richard Kaufmann. Another influential architect, Erich Mendelssohn, had his home and built houses there. Many university professors chose to reside next door to other university professors and intellectuals, hence S. Y. Agnon's description of Rehavia thus: "Doctor opposite Doctor they live."

The familiar German greeting, "Guten morgen, Herr Doktor", was as familiar in Jerusalem as it would be in Vienna or Berlin. I assume that Blum's visiting card term "Academic Painter" had something to do with the European titular complex. If any baker in Vienna is a "Bäckermeister", then a painter whose profession was acquired through hard study and work at an academy is definitely entitled to an academic title.

Fig. 6 Rehavia suburb

Architecturally, Rehavia's design was influenced by an influx of architects from the Bauhaus school in Dessau which was closed by the German authorities. Some reconciled themselves that they were expelled from their homes to their homeland, driven away from the cradle of

their mother tongue to the land of their forefathers.

Rehavia enjoyed a slower and quieter pace then the hustle and bustle of city life. The houses were surrounded by greenery and trees, keeping the sun out as much as possible. A typical Yekke house that I used to visit in my youth was so obsessed with excluding light that the shutters had to be kept down at all times. The switch, which is usually used to turn on a light, would be turned on in order to turn off the day and spread a gentle European darkness, a kind of yellowish half light.

Yekke Jerusalem was a city of cafés, of which the most famous were Café Veilchenfeld, Café Hermon, Café Rehavia and Café Taamon. Café Atara was in Ben Yehuda street (called Ben Yehuda Strasse by the Yekkes) as was Café Sichl, which was a popular meeting place for artists, writers and poets and a favourite haunt of the poet and artist Else Lasker-Schüler. Then there was the legendary Café Peter in the German Colony where the Jewish philosophers Martin Buber and Gershom Sholem were seen occasionally. Café Peter was just next to Erdmann's lime pit, which in the Templar community used to serve as a German "Bierkeller" (beer cellar).

S. Y. Agnon, the Israeli Nobel Literature Prize laureate wrote a particularly enchanting scene about Café Sichl. 'Shira (with her red turban) and Herbst' are sitting in a Jerusalem café. Enter the proprietor – elegantly dressed in a black suit with his close shave rendering his cheeks blue:

> Now that he had joined them he thought it would not be inappropriate for him to say a few words. He began telling about himself: that he is now here in Palestine and in Jerusalem that it had never occurred to him that he would come here, certainly not to live. "But," he continued, "Having come here, I wanted to set up a café like the one I had in Berlin. At first I thought I

would open a café in Tel Aviv, a dynamic city teeming with action. But when I saw the cafés there, half of which are out of doors, I decided against Tel Aviv. For, I, dear sir and dear madam, see the café as an enterprise that should offer refuge from the street rather than drag the street along with it. In Tel Aviv coffee drinkers sit outside, as if they are drinking soda, not coffee.[1]

A Yekke friend of mine recalls that his father, an ambassador, let his apartment to Ludwig Blum for what was to be his last studio after the Talitha Kumi building which housed his previous studio was demolished. The studio was in 42 King George Street in the heart of the city. The street name was retained by the municipality to commemorate the mandate's rule over Palestine. The studio was in one of two buildings built and owned by a Herr Fleischer where I was born and my connection with Ludwig Blum and his family grew.

Fig. 7 A plaque on King George Street

The studio's directions were east-west with two rather narrow arched windows facing east. They gave more than ample ("northern") light for the artist. Not long ago we were reminiscing about Blum and my friend remembered that he always finished three or four skies at a time, and then completed the urban or rural details, often using a photo of the scenery for reference. Blum captured the essence of that magnificent mosaic called Jerusalem.

In this Jerusalem, Ludwig Blum was the constant reminder of an artist in the old sense, of dignity in the old sense, of clothing and manners of the old world. When the Studio on King George Street was returned to the ambassador, Blum left behind a number of frames which I treasure as my part in Blum's history.

Karel Čapek, the Czech author, one time "Landsmann" (countryman) of Blum's, recommended the novice art collector to go for frames. Their prices tend to be more stable and you don't have to remain with the same painting all the time.

I have a few more arguments in favour of the option of settling for frames but I have far outstretched the frame of my remarks about Ludwig Blum's European Jerusalem.

Michael Dak

Jerusalem, September 2010

---

[1]   S.Y. Agnon, *Shira*, (1971) Trans. Zeva Shapiro, Syracuse University Press, 1996; Book 1, chapter 4.

Beyond

Self Portrait, 1920s
Watercolour and pencil on paper
34 x 25 cm

Fountain of Job, 1925, watercolour on paper, 22 x 33 cm

Tel Aviv under Construction, 1925, oil on canvas, 55 x 80 cm

Palmyra, Monumental Archway, 1930
Watercolour and pencil on paper
27.5 x 34 cm

Tehran, Dolat Gate, 1930
Watercolour and pencil on paper
26 x 35 cm

Women Laundering in the Tigris, Mosul, 1930, watercolour and pencil on paper, 19.5 x 27 cm

Kibbutz Kiryat Anavim, 1932, oil on canvas, 50 x 72 cm

Tiberias, 1934, oil on canvas, 61 x 105 cm

Purim Festival Street Decoration in Tel Aviv, c.1934-35, watercolour and pencil on paper, 27 x 36 cm

The Sand Dunes of Zur Shalom, Early 1940s, oil on canvas, 81 x 100 cm

Camels in the Judean Desert, 1943, oil on canvas, 80 x 130 cm

Tiberias, Tomb of Rabbi Meir Ba'al Haness, 1944, oil on canvas, 46.5 x 56 cm

Sunset in Tel Aviv, 1945, oil on canvas, 60 x 73 cm

Tel Aviv Promenade, 1946, oil on canvas, 51 x 74 cm

Pioneer Girl, 1947, oil on canvas, 50 x 60 cm

Water Tower in Kibbutz Negba, 1948
Oil on canvas
27 x 35 cm

Frank, Volunteer Solider from Canada, 1949
Oil on canvas
35 x 27 cm

Kibbutz Kfar Ruppin, 1950, oil on canvas, 11.5 x 16.8 cm

Haifa Bay, 1951, oil on canvas, 27.5 x 41 cm

Timna, Copper Mines, 1957, oil on canvas, 73 x 117 cm

A Mosque in Tiberias, 1964, oil on canvas, 27.5 x 35.5 cm

My Grandfather

Mira Chen

My Grandfather

Fig. 1 Blum at his studio in the Talitha Kumi building, Jerusalem, early 1950s

My maternal grandparents, Ludwig and Dina Blum, lived in Jerusalem since their arrival in Israel (then Palestine) – Dina in 1914, and Ludwig in 1923. They married in 1924, and my mother Dvora was born the same year, her brother Elie two years later. On graduating from highschool, both Dvora and Elie enlisted in the Palmach; Elie was killed in action in 1946.

My mother and my father, Shalom Hermon, married in 1947 and settled near Haifa, in Kiryat Tiv'on, where my two sisters and I were born and raised. Throughout our childhood, our grandparents were highly significant figures, visiting us at least twice a year and staying several days (at that period, the journey was long and tedious, taking several hours). We visited them too, taking the train to Jerusalem on our long school-holidays.

Some aspects of our visits to Jerusalem in the 1950s never changed. We always went to the Biblical Zoo and the Artists' House, and on Saturday afternoons we accompanied our grandparents to the King David Hotel where they met friends for coffee, while my sister and I roamed the hotel's lovely gardens.

We often joined Grandfather on his daily walk to his studio, which was then housed in the beautiful Talitha Kumi building (demolished in 1980, the Hamashbir department store now replaces it). A couple of beggars had a permanent pitch at a street-corner along our route, and Grandfather made sure that each of us had some small coins to give them.

Before starting the day's work in his studio, Grandfather would create a simple composition on the carpet – a vase of flowers, a bottle, or a pair of shoes – hoping that we would sit quietly and sketch a still-life. We loved watching him as he painted, whistling under his breath, or with a cigarette clamped at one side of his mouth. The most thrilling moment was when he completed a portrait, painting the white spot in the pupil of the eyes and instantly imbuing the features with life!

Fig. 2 *Portrait of Dina Mayer-Blum*, my Grandmother, 1944

A neighbour of mine once told me that when he was a child, his father had owned a plant nursery close to Talitha Kumi. Grandfather laid out his oil paintings to dry on the studio roof, and occasionally the breeze would send them fluttering down into the nursery. The child scooped up the paintings and ran to return them to Grandfather, who rewarded him with a few pennies. But when his father heard about it, he sent the child back, explaining, "We don't take money from Mr. Blum!".

Among my earliest memories is our annual trip to Gesher HaZiv situated between Naharia and Rosh Hanikra on 16 June, the date of the memorial for Elie and the Palmach fighters killed there. At the Nahariya bus station we met our grandparents, on their way to buy flowers, and then set off together for Gesher HaZiv. A memorial is still held there each year, and we attend it unfailingly.

I have many memories from our grandparents' visits to Tiv'on – Grandfather, always with a broad-brimmed hat, a black jacket with deep pockets that held a small sketchpad, pencil and brush, a box of watercolours and a tiny bottle of water, strolling though the garden or the street, halting now and then and 'framing' the view with his palms. When he came across an interesting object or composition he would stop, remove the sketchpad and execute a fast sketch. One such sketch – a flowering branch of pomegranate – still hangs in my home.

There was a climbing frame in our garden. When our grandparents arrived, as soon as he put down their suitcases my grandfather would perform some exercises on the horizontal bar. His particular expertise was the 'sun' exercise – 360 degree turns – which he had performed as a young man at Maccabi sports meetings in Europe.

During the Blum exhibition at Beit Hatfutsot in 2009, I met dozens of people who remembered him fondly, many with paintings that they had acquired or inherited, and heard their moving accounts. There was the lady from Jerusalem who described her mother's knitwear salon in downtown Jerusalem. One day in the 1940s, the artist Ludwig Blum entered the shop and suggested to her mother that he would paint a portrait of her and her daughter, in exchange for four knitted sweaters. The paintings are now in the daughter's possession. Another elderly woman told me about her friend's children who turned up at Ludwig's studio clutching their money-boxes and a photo of their parents – to request a painting for the parents' wedding anniversary. Naturally, he complied. In a moshav near Netanya, there are many residents originally from Czechoslovakia, one of whom was a good friend of Blum. In the 1950s, Blum was in financial straits for a while. His friend organised a sale of Blum's work in the moshav, and many members purchased paintings. I also heard about that family's annual winter vacations spent with the Blums in a Sea of Galilee hotel. On each visit, Blum would leave a painting in exchange for their stay at the hotel … which explains the large body of paintings that depict Tiberias and the lake in winter!

I met many families of Czech and German origin whose parents had purchased paintings by Blum in the 1920s and 1930s and had managed to escape from Europe to Palestine by 1938, bringing the pictures with them. One such was the adopted daughter of Mr. Lachs, an affluent Czech industrialist from Brno, who had bought many paintings from Blum before World War II, but couldn't get out of Europe in time. The Nazis confiscated all his possessions, and deported his wife and children to the gas chambers. In an amazing chain of events, Lachs survived and ultimately reached Israel, where he began a new life, from scratch. During the 1950s he visited Blum in his studio. Grandfather was thrilled to see him again, and after listening to his account forced him to choose a painting from those on the wall and take it home – "Pay me when you can".

Fig. 3 My mother Dvora Herman-Blum and her three daughters by the Jerusalem Panorama, Gregor Mendel Museum, Brno, October, 2000

Fig. 4 Blum speaking at the opening of an exhibition

In a similar vein, I heard from the renowned chemist and pharmacist Dr. Rose Bilbool, who celebrated her 100th birthday in 2010. A neighbour and close friend of the Blums in the 1940s, she was an art-lover though not well-off at the time. She was enchanted by a painting of three figures on a street in the Old City – a Jew, an Arab, and a Christian priest – that she had seen at an exhibition. Dr. Bilbool longed to buy it, but its price was seven times higher than her monthly salary. In the end, Blum gave her a discount, and she repaid it in 24 monthly instalments.

Another of Blum's neighbours, a woman of English extraction, paid a visit of several months to her homeland. On her return, she heard that Blum's son Elie had been killed. She went to the Blum home to pay a condolence visit, bringing a bunch of anemones with her. As she was about to leave, Grandfather went to the next room and returned with a small painting of two anemones, and gave it to her.

We met an elderly woman in whose house hangs a portrait of her grandmother, painted in 1923. She told us that her parents and grandmother lived together in Migdal, on the Sea of Galilee. Ludwig Blum lived in their house for several days, while he roamed the region and painted landscapes. Unable to pay rent for his lodging, he suggested that he paint a portrait of the family's infant. The mother replied: "This baby will be painted by lots of artists … I'd prefer you to paint my mother". And so it was. It was fascinating to see the strong resemblance between the painting on the wall and the granddaughter today!

Mira Chen

Ludwig Blum's eldest granddaughter

CATALOGUE OF WORKS & TOPOGRAPHICAL NOTES

Listed in chronological order: dimensions are in centimetres, height before width

Self Portrait
1920s
Watercolour and pencil on paper
34 x 25

Family of the Artist Collection

This painting dates from around the time that Ludwig Blum immigrated to Palestine, married his wife Dina and had his two children Elie and Dvora. This portrait represents a time of great change in Blum's life and the beginning of his paintings of the "land of light and promise".

Jerusalem, View from Mount Scopus towards the Valley of Jehoshaphat
1924
Oil on canvas
Signed, titled and dated bottom left
49 x 59

Private collection

Jerusalem is viewed from Mount Scopus, probably from the site of the Hebrew University looking westward. The south-east corner of the Old City wall, with the Temple Mount buildings can be observed on the left. The foreground shows an agricultural terrain, dotted with olive groves of the Valley of Jehoshaphat, commonly known as Wadi Joz. Today this area is a densely populated neighbourhood of East Jerusalem.

Fountain of Job
1925
Watercolour on paper
Signed, titled and dated bottom right
22 x 33

Private collection

This composition shows a remarkable similarity to an 1843 lithograph of the same title by David Roberts. The positions of the three figures in the foreground, repeating those in Roberts', disclose Blum's debt to the Scottish artist.

Tel Aviv under Construction
1925
Oil on canvas
Signed, titled and dated bottom left
55 x 80

Private collection

Tel Aviv, which was known as the First Hebrew City, played an important role in the Zionist enterprise. The large structure seen in the middle ground under construction may be the High School of Commerce built in the mid 1920s.

Jerusalem, inside the Walls, Looking East
1926
Oil on canvas
Signed and dated bottom left
81 x 140

Stern family collection

The artist probably stood on the roof of the Petra Hotel near the Jaffa Gate looking towards the Mount of Olives and Mount Scopus. From this viewpoint the dome of the synagogue called Hurva (lit. The Ruin), in the Jewish Quarter by the right edge of the picture, is seen higher than the Dome of the Rock in the centre. The Arab houses are topped with stone domes alongside the European influenced tiled roof houses which developed rapidly during the 19th century mainly in the Christian Quarter. The added balconies in the foreground are evidence of the constant changes in the city's architecture.

CATALOGUE OF WORKS & TOPOGRAPHICAL NOTES

Walls of Jerusalem
1926
Oil on canvas
Signed and dated bottom right
40 x 50

Collection of Yossi and Daniela Lipschitz

As often in Blum's landscapes the site is specific and accurately portrayed. The composition depicts the north-eastern section of the wall not far from Gethsemane and a Muslim cemetery can be observed at the top right side.

Jerusalem in Snow
1927
Oil on canvas
Signed, titled and dated Latin bottom left
Signed and Hebrew bottom centre
41 x 61

Private collection

Blum painted this work from Mount Scopus with the Valley of Kidron clearly visible on the left and the olive trees in the foreground. Blum painted out of doors all year round.

This was the first snow that Ludwig Blum had seen since he had settled in the city in 1923.

Church of the Holy Sepulchre
1928
Oil on canvas
Signed, titled and dated bottom right
38 x 46

Private collection

The Church of the Holy Sepulchre, located inside the walled Old City, was first built in the 4th century on the site of the crucifixion and burial of Jesus. The Romanesque arched façade, seen in this picture, was built during the Crusader period and is the only outer view of the Church. The vantage point hides the receding domes much as the pilgrims and visitors see it today.

Jerusalem, Temple Mount
1928
Oil on canvas
Signed, titled and dated bottom left
33 x 45

Private collection

The Dome of the Rock at the centre of the Temple Mount is the most universally recognisable symbol of Jerusalem. Blum dedicated several paintings to a close-up view of the Temple Mount's major shrines seen from a high point in the Jewish Quarter. The Dome of the Rock rises high at the centre as the focus of the composition. Its dome was clad in darkened lead in those days. Today it is golden thanks to a generous donation of King Hussein of Jordan in 1998 and 80kg of gold that cover it.

Grove of Olives, Gethsemane
1928–30
Oil on canvas mounted on cardboard
Signed Latin and Hebrew and dated
1930 bottom left
Signed, titled and dated Latin 1928
bottom right
31.5 x 46

Private collection

Gethsemane, one of the Christian holy places in Jerusalem, was where Jesus prayed shortly before his arrest.

"The Garden of Olives" is about 1,200 sq. m. and is situated at the foot of the Mount of Olives in Jerusalem.

Palmyra, Monumental Archway
1930
Watercolour and pencil on paper
Signed, titled and dated bottom left
27.5 x 34

Family of the Artist Collection

In August 1930, Ludwig Blum accompanied Dr. Wolfgang von Weisel in his mission to Kurdistan, to report on the Kurdish rebellion against Turkey. The following three works date from this journey.

Located 215km northeast of Damascus, Palmyra – or Tadmor – was a city in ancient Syria. Many of the ruins remaining at the site date from the Greco-Roman period.

Tehran, Dolat Gate
1930
Watercolour and pencil on paper
Signed, titled and dated bottom left
26 x 35

Family of the Artist Collection

Tehran was surrounded by six gates of which Dolat Gate was one. Dolat Gate was not accessible to the general public, which explains the lack of people in the foreground of this painting. Had it been one of the other gates into Tehran the scene would have been busier.

Women laundering at the Tigris, Mosul
1930
Watercolour and pencil on paper
Signed, titled and dated bottom left
19.5 x 27

Family of the Artist Collection

The Tigris is one of Iraq's two main rivers and stretches 1,850 km from the Taurus Mountains in eastern Turkey to its confluence with the Euphrates near Basra. The Tigris was once used as a major trading route, but, as over-ground transportation improved in the late 19th century, it became once again a place where women from the region would come to wash their clothes. As well as Mosul, cities Along the Tigris include Baghdad, Basra and Nineveh.

CATALOGUE OF WORKS & TOPOGRAPHICAL NOTES

Kibbutz Kiryat Anavim
1932
Oil on canvas
Signed, titled and dated bottom left
50 x 72

Lerer Family collection, Israel

Kiryat Anavim was the first Kibbutz settled in the Judean Hills. Located 12 km from Jerusalem, 50 km from Tel Aviv and 650 m above sea level, the land was initially bought in 1913-14 from the Effendi of Abu Gosh by the Zionist Organisation, Histadrut Hatzionit. In 1919, settlers from the Ukraine established the Kibbutz.

Kibbutz Degania
1934
Oil on canvas
Signed, titled and dated bottom left
50 x 60

Private collection

Kibbutz Degania was the first Kibbutz settlement, founded in 1910. The land, located southwest of Lake Kinnereth, was bought by the Jewish National Fund. The 'Big House' as it was known, seen in the background, was built behind the cypress tree in 1921 as residence for the unmarried Kibbutz members. It was so massive that it survived unscathed the 1927 earthquake.

Tiberias
1934
Oil on canvas
61 x 105

Collection of WIZO London

Tiberias is a city on the western shore of the Sea of Galilee, established in 20CE, it was named in honour of the emperor Tiberius. Today the population numbers 41,300 making it the commercial and religious centre of Northern Israel.

Mural Sketch for the Jerusalem Artists' Ball
c. 1934
Watercolour and pencil on paper
27 x 47

Family of the Artist Collection

This picture was designed as a mural decoration for the Purim Ball of the Jerusalem artists hence the artistic theme at its centre. The artist, dressed in an oriental costume is watched by a British soldier, an Arab man and a donkey while painting the landscape of Jerusalem. The grid of pencil lines was the preparation for enlarging the picture. There is no record of this or similar sketches being executed as paintings.

Purim Festival Street Decoration in Tel Aviv
c. 1934–5
Watercolour and pencil on paper
27 x 36

Family of the Artist Collection

The Jewish festival of Purim commemorates G-d's deliverance of the Jews of the Persian Empire from massacre by Haman, Viceroy of King Ahasuerus; the story is recounted in the biblical Book of Esther. This work depicts Purim being celebrated in the 1930s in Tel Aviv. The decorative arches shown did not survive and, apart from a few black and white photographs, this painting is a rare record of them.

The Sand Dunes of Zur Shalom
Early 1940s
Oil on canvas
Signed Latin and Hebrew bottom left
81 x 100

Private collection

Zur Shalom is an area of sand dunes along Israel's Mediterranean coast. It is located southwest of Kfar Masaryk between Acre and Haifa.

Camels in the Judean Desert
1943
Oil on canvas
Signed and dated Latin bottom left
Signed and dated Hebrew bottom right
80 x 130

Private collection

A day's work on Mount Scopus would start in the morning when Blum would turn westward, the light on his back, and paint the Old City. In the afternoon, as the sun set in the west, he turned his easel eastward to paint the desert, the Dead Sea and the pinkish mountains of Moab seen in the background.

Temple Mount and the Western Wall
1943
Oil on canvas
Signed and dated Latin bottom left
Signed Hebrew bottom right
32 x 46

Private collection

The octagonal building, the earliest existing Islamic monument (completed 692 CE) was built on a sacred rock upon which the Prophet Muhammad is believed to have stepped when rising to the Heavens and receiving guidance from God. The Foundation Stone in Jewish tradition is considered to be the site of the Holy of Holies of the Jewish Temple (destroyed 70 CE).

CATALOGUE OF WORKS & TOPOGRAPHICAL NOTES

Jerusalem, View from Mount Scopus
1944
Oil on canvas
Signed, titled and dated bottom right
33.5 x 60

Private collection

This 1944 panoramic view of Jerusalem was painted from Mount Scopus. When compared to the 1949 view of the city similarly from Mount Scopus (see p. 40) the diversity of Jerusalem's climate becomes apparent.

This painting captures the arid desert-like terrain of the summer compared to the rich fertile grounds of Spring vividly depicted in the later view.

Tiberias, Tomb of Rabbi Meir Ba'al Haness
1944
Oil on canvas
Signed and dated Latin bottom left
Signed Hebrew bottom right
46.5 x 56

Private collection

According to some traditions this tomb on the shore of the Sea of Galilee is the burial site of the famous sage Rabbi Meir (2nd Century CE) called Ba'al Haness ('the miracle maker'). It has long been a Jewish pilgrimage site and in the 19th century a synagogue and Yeshivas (religious colleges) were built there.

Sunset in Tel Aviv
1945
Oil on canvas
Signed, titled and dated Latin bottom left
Signed Hebrew bottom right
60 x 73

Private collection

Sea views are often at the heart of compositions from the European Romanticism and Impressionist periods but seldom found in 20th century art from Israel. This view seen from the sea shore of Tel Aviv is somewhat unusual even in the repertoire of Ludwig Blum who painted Tel Aviv several times throughout his career.

Tel Aviv Promenade
1946
Oil on canvas
Signed Latin bottom left
Signed, titled and dated Hebrew bottom right
51 x 74

Private collection

The seashore has been an important part of Tel Aviv's social life and leisure since the 1920s, with bustling cafés and crowded beaches.

This is a modern scene of the Tel Aviv 'Riviera' along the Herbert Samuel Quay, which was named after the first British High Commissioner. It was an elevated promenade separated from the bathing area that was opened in 1939.

Pioneer Girl
1947
Oil on canvas
Signed and dated Latin bottom left
Signed Hebrew bottom right
50 x 60

Private collection, bequest of Anieta &
Reuven Sharie

The painting shows a young woman at work feeding chickens in one of the Zionist settlements, probably a Kibbutz in the Valley Jezre'el. The female pioneer is characteristically dressed in shorts and blue short sleeves blouse with head scarf and her exposed skin is tanned from her long hours working in the sun.

Jerusalem, Notre Dame in Ruins
1948
Oil on canvas
Signed and dated, Latin bottom left
Signed and dated Hebrew bottom right
60.5 x 50

Family of the Artist Collection

This painting shows the church in the destroyed southern wing of the hostel that became the front line for Israeli soldiers facing the Old City's rampart. The pilgrim centre, now called Notre Dame of Jerusalem, remained under Israeli authority after 1948 and was restored in the 1970s. The ruined church never returned to its original function.

Jerusalem, view from British Government Palace (Armon Hanatziv)
1948
Oil on canvas
Signed and dated Latin bottom left
Signed and dated Hebrew bottom right
59 x 72

Dubi Shiff Collection, Tel Aviv

This view is from the south (opposite to the view from Mount Scopus) from *Armon Hanatziv* (palace of the [high] commissioner) – the Government House. The Kidron Valley and its steep cliff just below the city wall are clearly visible in the centre.

Water Tower in Kibbutz Negba
1948
Oil on canvas
Signed Latin bottom left
Signed, titled and dated Hebrew
bottom right
27 x 35

Family of the Artist Collection

Founded in 1939, Kibbutz Negba, to the east of Ashkelon, was the southernmost Jewish settlement in the Negev desert during the British Mandate. Negba suffered almost total destruction in the 1948 Arab-Israeli war / War of Independence during heavy fighting.

CATALOGUE OF WORKS & TOPOGRAPHICAL NOTES

Frank, Volunteer Soldier from Canada
1949
Oil on canvas
35 x 27

Private collection

Frank would have been one of around 4,000 volunteers from all over the world who came to fight on the Israeli side during the Arab-Israeli War / War of Independence in 1948. This is a portrait of one amongst many men, who came from beyond Palestine to fight for the establishment of the state of Israel.

Jerusalem, view from Mount Scopus
1949
Oil on canvas
Signed and titled Latin bottom left
Signed, titled and dated Hebrew bottom right
73 x 116

Private collection

In addition to the Dome of the Rock on the left, one can notice at the centre back the black cone-shaped roof of the Dormition Church, built in the early 20th century on Mount Zion. The Rockefeller Museum of Archaeology, the elongated yellowish building seen by the right edge of the canvas, was built in the 1930s by the British Mandatory Government of Palestine and designed by its Chief Architect, Austen St. Barbe Harrison.

Kibbutz Kfar Ruppin
1950
Oil on canvas
Signed and dated Hebrew bottom left
11.5 x 16.8

Family of the Artist Collection

Kibbutz Kfar Ruppin is located in the Beit She'an Valley in northern Israel. It was founded in 1938 by immigrants from Germany, Bohemia and Austria.

Haifa Bay
1951
Oil on canvas
27.5 x 41

Family of the Artist Collection

Haifa bay is fed by the Kishon river and it is situated between Haifa and Acre. It is Israel's only natural harbour.

Timna, Copper Mines
1957
Oil on canvas
73 x 117
Signed and dated Latin bottom left
Signed and titled Hebrew bottom left

Private collection

Blum was the first, perhaps the only Israeli artist to pay attention to industrial projects and landscapes as part of his desire to chronicle the pioneering spirit of the early years of the State of Israel, creating a rare historical document of this project in is initial stages.

Jerusalem, View of Sultan's Pool and the Citadel
1960
Oil on canvas
Signed and dated Latin and Hebrew bottom left
50 x 73

Stern Gallery, Tel Aviv

Between 1948 and 1967 Israelis' viewing points of the Old City were limited to the border zones in the western part of the city. Blum probably painted this from a hill above the Valley of Hinnom known as Bible Hill, where today the Menachem Begin Heritage Centre is sited. The dam bridge across the painting's foreground allowed the creation of the reservoir named after the Ottoman Sultans who rebuilt it. In the middle ground, Arab-Jewish neighbourhoods that remained abandoned in the no-man's-land following the 1948 War of Independence are to be seen. In the background are the minaret of the Citadel on the right and the tower of the Latin Patriarchy on the left.

Mea She'arim neighbourhood, Jerusalem; View of Ein Ya'akov Street
1960
Oil on canvas
Signed and dated Latin bottom left
Signed Hebrew bottom centre
61 x 46

Private collection

After 1948 with no access to this part of Jerusalem, Blum made several replicas of his Old City scenes. By the early 1960s he found appropriate substitutes in the 19th century neighbourhoods of Mea She'arim and Nahalat Shiv'a, and street markets in west Jerusalem.

A Mosque in Tiberias
1964
Oil on canvas
Signed and dated Latin bottom centre
Signed Hebrew bottom right
27.5 x 35.5

Family of the Artist Collection

This mosque is one of the few remains of the Muslim section of Tiberias, mostly destroyed in the 1948 War. The El Omri mosque was built in 1743 by Daher el-Omar, the Arab-Bedouin ruler of the Galilee district of the Ottoman Empire. He was best known for his building and fortifications in Tiberias, Acre and Haifa. He invited the Jews to return to Tiberias and rebuilt its Jewish quarter and both communities lived side by side. El Omri was inspired by the famous Hagia Sofia mosque in Istanbul but built in the black basalt stone typical of Tiberias. The mosque features on a stamp, one of four views of Palestine, issued by the British Mandate in 1927.

Figures Reproduced in Essays

Portrait of a Country: Ludwig Blum Paints the Land of Light and Promise: Dr. Dalia Manor, Curator of the Exhibition

Fig. 1 *Self Portrait,* 1920s, watercolour and pencil on paper, 34 x 25 cm, private collection

Fig. 2 Ludwig Blum in uniform of the Austro-Hungarian Army, c. 1918

Fig. 3 Ludwig Blum with fellow gymnasts (second from the right), 1920

Fig. 4 *Jerusalem, Damascus Gate,* 1928, oil on canvas, 27 x 35 cm, private collection

Fig. 5 Ludwig Blum works on the Jerusalem Panorama, 1937

Fig. 6 *Jerusalem, View from the Mount of Olives,* 1936, oil on canvas, 50 x 188 cm, private collection

Fig. 7 *Portrait of Sir John Chancellor, The High Commissioner,* 1930, oil on canvas, 73 x 60 cm, Collection of Susanna Johnston, Dumfries, Scotland

Fig. 8 *View of the Dead Sea,* 1945, oil on canvas, 35 x 70 cm, collection of Daphna and Joram Weidenfeld

Fig. 9 John Singer Sargent, *The Mountains of Moab,* 1905, oil on canvas, 65.4 x 111 cm, Tate, London 2010

Fig. 10 *Portrait of Dvora, the artist's daughter aged fifteen, 1939, oil on canvas, 98.5 x 78 cm*

Fig. 11 David Bomberg, *Jerusalem, Looking to Mount Scopus,* 1925, oil on canvas, 56.5 x 75.2 cm Tate, London 2010

Fig. 12 *Jerusalem, inside the Walls, Looking East,* 1926, oil on canvas, signed and dated bottom left, 81 x 140 cm, Stern family collection

Fig. 13 *Tel Aviv, View towards Jaffa,* 1927, oil on canvas, 60 x 107 cm, private collection

Fig. 14 David Roberts, *Fountain of Job Valley of Hinnom,* 1842, lithograph, from: *The Holy Land, Syria, Idumea, Arabia, Egypt and Nubia,* lithographed by Louis Haghe, London: F.G. Moon, 1842 1845, v. 1, p. 6.

Fig. 15 *Fountain of Job,* 1925, watercolour on paper, 22 x 33 cm, private collection

Fig. 16 Model in the artist's studio, 1920s

Fig. 17 *Frank, Volunteer Soldier from Canada,* 1949, oil on canvas, 35 x 27 cm, private collection

Fig. 18 The artist in his shell-damaged studio, 1948

Fig. 19 *Nazareth,* 1958, oil on canvas, 60 x 50 cm, private collection

Fig. 20 *Haifa Bay,* 1951, oil on canvas, 27.5 x 41 cm, private collection

Fig. 21 Ludwig Blum paints Mount Zion and the walls of the Old City of Jerusalem, 1930

The European Jerusalem of Ludwig Blum: Michael Dak

Fig. 1 Viennese café scene

Fig. 2 Theodor Herzl

Fig. 3 Franz Kafka

Fig. 4 Gustav Mahler

Fig. 5 Erich Mendelssohn, Hebrew University, Hadassah Medical Center, Mt. Scopus, Jerusalem

Fig. 6 Rehavia suburb

Fig. 7 A plaque on King George Street

My Grandfather: Mira Chen

Fig. 1 Blum at his studio in the Talitha Kumi building, Jerusalem, early 1950s

Fig. 2 *Portrait of Dina Mayer-Blum,* the artist's wife, 1944, oil on canvas, 100 x 60cm

Fig. 3 My mother Dvora Herman-Blum and her three daughters by the Jerusalem Panorama, Gregor Mendel Museum, Brno, October, 2000

Fig. 4 Blum speaking at the opening of an exhibition

Bibliography & Further Reading

Newman, Elias, *Art in Palestine,* New York: Siebel Company Publisher, 1939

Gamzu, Dr Chaim, *Painting and Sculpture in Israel,* Tel Aviv: Eshcol Publishers, 1951

Roth, Cecil, *Jewish Art, an Illustrated History,* London: Valentine Mitchell, 1971

Goodman, Susan Tumarkin, *Artists of Israel 1920 1980,* New York: Jewish Museum, Wayne State University Press, 1981

Shilo-Cohen, Nurit, *Bezalel 1906 1929,* Jerusalem: The Israel Museum, 1983

Kampf, Avram, *Jewish Experience in the Art of the Twentieth Century,* Connecticut: Bergin & Garvey Publishers, 1984

Gahnassia, Yael, *Ludwig Blum 1891 1974,* Jerusalem: Mayanot Art Gallery & Publishers, 1988

Rubin, Carmela and Naftali, Shiri, *Catalogue of the Permanent Collection,* Tel Aviv: Rubin Museum, 1993

Arbel, Rachel, *Blue & White in Color Visual Images of Zionism, 1897 1947,* Tel Aviv: Beit Hatfutsot, the Nahum Goldmann Museum of the Jewish Diaspora, 1996

Ofrat, Gideon, *One Hundred Years of Art in Israel,* Boulder: Westview Press, 1998

Omer, Mordechai (ed.), *90 Years of Israeli Art: A Selection from the Joseph Hackmey - Israel Phoenix Collection,* Tel Aviv: Tel Aviv Museum of Art, 1998

Simoen, Jean-Claude, *Le Voyage en Terre Sainte,* Paris: Impact Livre, 2000

LeVitte-Harten, Doreet, *Die Neuen Hebräer: 100 Jahre Kunst in Israel,* Berlin: Nicolai Verlag, 2005

Manor, Dalia, *Art in Zion: The Genesis of Modern National Art in Jewish Palestine,* London: Routledge, 2005

Rubin, Carmela, *Reuven Rubin Dreamland,* Tel Aviv: Tel Aviv Museum of Art, 2006

Hermann Struck 1876-1944, Berlin: Stiftung Neue Synagogue Berlin / Open Museum Israel, 2007

Bar Or, Galia and Ofrat, Gideon, *The First Decade: A Hegemony and a Plurality,* Ein Harod: Museum of Art, 2008

Benjamin, Chaya, *Early Israeli Arts & Crafts,* Jerusalem: Israel Museum, 2008

Glasser, David, *Israel & Art, 60 Years through the eyes of Teddy Kollek,* London: Ben Uri, London Jewish Museum of Art, 2008

Bar Or, Galia, *A Selection of Israeli Art from the Collection of Gaby and Ami Brown,* Ein Harod: Museum of Art, 2009

Manor, Dalia, *The Real and the Ideal: The Painting of Ludwig Blum,* Tel Aviv: Beit Hatfutsot Museum, 2009

Solo Exhibitions

| 1925 | Artists' House in Brno, Czechoslovakia |

1925   Artists' House in Brno, Czechoslovakia

1927   Tourism Club of Eretz Yisrael, Tel Aviv Jewish Town Hall, Prague

1928   *Palestine in Pictures*, Teplice Museum Czechoslovakia

1929   J.S Fetter & Co., Amsterdam; Neue Kunsthandlung, Berlin

1930   Slovak Artistic Forum, Bratislava

1932   Palace Moravia, Brno

1933   Wertheim Gallery, London

1934   Steimatzky Gallery, Jerusalem

1938   Home of Mrs. Ben Zion Halper, London

        Paintings of Jerusalem, with Abel Pann: Bible Characters and Scenes, The Fine Art Society, London

1944   Menorah Club, Jerusalem

1951–52 Exhibitions in Jewish and Christian congregations, New York

1952   Beryl Lush Gallery, Philadelphia

1960   *La Terre Sainte par Ludwig Blum*, Galerie Marcel Bernheim, Paris

1963   Retrospective Exhibition, *Forty Years in Eretz Israel*, Artists' House, Jerusalem

1967   Retrospective Exhibition, *Ludwig Blum at 75*, Artists' House, Jerusalem

1973   Jubilee Exhibition Jerusalem

1982   *Jerusalem – War and Peace*, Yad Labanim House, Jerusalem

1987   *Ludwig Blum: A Portrait of a Period – Jerusalem 1948*, the Tourjeman Post, Jerusalem

        Blum in 1948, The Knesset (The Israeli Parliament)

1988   *Ludwig Blum, 1891–1974*, Mayanot Gallery, Jerusalem

1995   *Ludwig Blum: Paintings*, Moravian Gallery, Brno

        Jerusalem of Ludwig Blum, Franz Kafka Centre, Prague

1998   *In Be'er Sheva and in and in the Negev– The Painter Ludwig Blum*, Yad Labanim House, Be'er Sheva

2004   *Paintbrush and Recollection: Ludwig Blum Paints the Struggle for Independence*, The Palmach Museum, Tel Aviv

2009   *The Real and the Ideal: The Painting of Ludwig Blum*, Beit Hatfutsot Museum, Tel Aviv

2011   *The Land of Light and Promise: 50 Years Painting Jerusalem and Beyond*, Ben Uri, The London Jewish Museum of Art, London

Group Exhibitions

1924–28   Annual exhibitions of the Jewish Artists Association at the Citadel, Jerusalem

1930   Exhibition of the 19th and 20th century Jewish Artists, Fénix Palace, Prague

1932   *Artists of Jerusalem,* Tower of David, Jerusalem

1934   *The Portrait in Palestine,* The National Museum Bezalel, Jerusalem

1936   Exhibition of Palestinian Artists, Tel Aviv Museum

1938   Royal Academy of Arts, London

Annual Exhibition of the Ben Uri Art Society, London

1941   General Exhibition of Palestine Artists, HaBima Theatre

1942   Cabinet of Arts (Schlosser Gallery), Jerusalem

1945   Exhibition of Palestine Artist, Tel Aviv

1946   Exhibition of Palestine Artist, Tel Aviv

1949   *Artists of Jerusalem,* Artists' House, Jerusalem

1950   *The Sea in Art,* Artists' House, Jerusalem

1952   Israeli Arts Festival, Beth El Community Center, New Rochelle, New York

1957   Spring Exhibition, The Jerusalem Artists Association, Artists' House, Jerusalem

1958   *Ten Years of Painting and Sculpture,* The Jerusalem Artists Association, Artists' House, Jerusalem

1965   *Israeli Artists Exhibition: Tower of David Period,* Ministry of Education and the American-

Israel Cultural Foundation, travelling exhibition

1969   Festival of Painting and Sculpture, Exhibition Gardens, Tel Aviv

1984   *Landscapes in Israeli Art: 100 years of Creation,* President of Israel Residence, Jerusalem

1986   *Color Territories,* Israel Pavilion, the Venice Biennale

1987   *The Golden Age of Safed Landscapes,* Museum of Art, Ein Harod

1988   *1948: The War of Independence in Israeli Art,* Eretz Israel Museum, Tel Aviv

Upon One of the Mountains – Jerusalem in Israeli Art, The Genia Schreiber University Art Gallery, Tel Aviv University

1992   *Jerusalem – Before the Gold,* Municipal Art Gallery, Rehovot

1993   Works from the Collection, Petach Tikva Museum

At the Sea of Galilee: Paintings by Israeli artists, Bet Gabriel on the Kinneret, Israel

1996   *Windows,* The Israel Museum, Jerusalem

1997   *Left–Right,* Gordon Gallery, Tel Aviv

1998   *90 Years of Israeli Art; a Selection from the Joseph Hackmey – Israel Phoenix Collection,* Tel Aviv Museum of Art, Tel Aviv

2002   *The Return to Zion, Beyond the Principle of Locality,* Zman LeOmanut Gallery, Tel Aviv

Group Exhibitions contd.

2003   *Ruins Revisited, IMAGES OF Ruins in Israel, 1803–2003*, Zman LeOmanut Gallery, Tel Aviv

2004   *Our Landscape: Notes on Landscape Painting in Israel*, Art Gallery, Haifa University

2005   *Die Neuen Hebräer: 100 Jahre Kunst in Israel*, Martin-Gropius-Bau, Berlin

2006   *Miron Sima and Friends*, Isaac Kaplan Old Yishuv Court Museum, Jerusalem

2008   *1948: 'Hebrew, Eretz-Israeli Art Leading to the Future', Museum of Art, Ein Harod*

        The First Decade: A Hegemony and a Plurality, Museum of Art, Ein Harod

        'A Woman of Valor Who Can Find' Images of Women Fighters during the State Foundation, Negev Museum of Art, Be'er Sheva

Public Collections

The Jewish Museum in Prague; The Israel Museum, Jerusalem; Tel Aviv Museum of Art; Petach-Tikva Museum of Art; Museum of Art, Ein Harod; The Open Museum, Tefen Industrial Park; Bar David Museum of Jewish Art and Judaica, Kibbutz Bar-Am; Jabotinsky Museum, Tel Aviv; The Negev Museum of Art

Patrons

Gretha Arwas
Pauline and Daniel Auerbach
Esther and Simon Bentley
Miriam and Richard Borchard
Barry Cann
Marion and David Cohen
Sheila and Dennis Cohen Charitable Trust
Nikki and Mel Corin
Suzanne and Henry Davis
Rachel and Mike Dickson
Peter Dineley
Marion and Manfred Durst
The Fidelio Charitable Trust
H W Fisher and Company
Wendy Fisher
The Foyle Foundation
Franklin family
Barbara and David Glass
Sue and David Glasser
Lindy and Geoffrey Goldkorn
Madelaine and Craig Gottlieb
Averil and Irving Grose
Tresnia and Gideon Harbour
Mym and Lawrence Harding
Peter Held
Morven and Michael Heller
Beverley and Tony Jackson
Jewish Memorial Council
Joan Hurst
Sandra and John Joseph
Annely Juda Fine Art
Neil Kitchener QC
Tamar Kollek
Hannah and David Latchman

Agnes and Edward Lee
Pamela and Michael Lester
Hannah Lowy and Lord Mitchell
Montgomery Gallery, San Francisco
Jacob Mendelson Scholarship Trust
Hugh Merrell
Robin and Edward Milstein
Diana and Allan Morgenthau
Mishcon de Reya
MutualArt.com
Susan and Leo Noe
Opera Gallery, London
Osborne Samuel Gallery, London
Susan and Martin Paisner
Shoshana and Benjamin Perl
Ingrid and Mike Posen
Simon Posen
Janis and Barry Prince
Reed Smith LLP
Ashley Rogoff
Anthony Rosenfelder
Rothschild Foundation (Europe)
Blick Rothenberg
Shoresh Charitable Trust
Lélia Pissarro and David Stern
Ann Susman
Esther and Romie Tager
Myra Waiman
Judit and George Weisz
Cathy Wills
Alma and Leslie Wolfson
Sylvie and Saul Woodrow
Matt Yeoman

International Advisory Board